I0528837

WISDOM

STILL

SHOUTS

WISDOM
STILL
SHOUTS

A CALL FOR THE PASTOR'S USE OF WISDOM LITERATURE IN DISCIPLESHIP

Scott Corbin

NEBP
NORTHEASTERN BAPTIST PRESS
Bennington, Vermont

Wisdom Still Shouts

A Call for the Pastor's Use of Wisdom Literature in Discipleship

Copyright © 2023 by Scott Corbin

Published by Northeastern Baptist Press
        Post Office Box 4600
        Bennington, VT 05201

All rights reserved. No part of this book may be reproduced in any form without prior permission from Northeastern Baptist Press, except as provided for by USA copyright law.

Scripture quotations taken from the (NASB®) New American Standard Bible®. Copyright © 1960, 1971, 1977, 1995, 2020 by The Lockman Foundation. Used by permission. All rights reserved. *www.lockman.org*

Softcover ISBN: 978-1-953331-31-1

To Barbi, my prudent wife of precious value,
my own good gift and favor from the LORD.
(Prov 18:22)

TABLE OF CONTENTS

FOREWORD
by
Mark McGinniss

We are living at a time in Church history where the Old Testament has been undervalued, unappreciated and even by some "unhitched" from the modern church. Fortunately, Scott's book challenges the current trends and recognizes the healthy value of the OT. He appreciates that it still speaks to the Church in our present day and culture. Far from "unhitching" the OT from the pulpit, Scott offers a clarion call for pastors to embrace its wisdom anew.

But Scott's call to pastors is a specific one—it is a call for pastors to utilize the wisdom literature of the OT for discipling today's believers. While some may scoff at turning to Proverbs, Ecclesiastes, Job and even the Song of Songs for training NT saints, Scott makes a compelling case, and the Apostle Paul in 2 Timothy 3:15–17 provides ample NT evidence that his premise is correct.

As a pastor himself, Scott understands the absolute necessity of discipling believers in the whole counsel of God. He handles well the often-neglected wisdom literature of the OT. He challenges and shows pastors how these wise sacred texts will go a long way in producing well-grounded and well-rounded disciples of Jesus Christ.

This book is much like Lady Wisdom in Proverbs—it shouts to all who want to make disciples or simply to be better disciples, to heed her call to be wise. And this wisdom is so desperately needed by modern disciples to navigate this life well. For surely, it shouldn't take much convincing that unless we respond to the many obstacles that this world proffers daily in which we are but sojourners, we will suffer like so many the shipwreck of our faith and lives. Pastor Scott understands that godly wisdom for such life and death challenges are found in the OT Wisdom Literature, and he pilots, for all wise believers, a course on how to use these God inspired OT texts well.

Like Lady Wisdom, Scott's book "shouts" over the many voices and noisy internet opinions that suggest the OT is obsolete, irrelevant and an embarrassment to the church. This book is the wise voice that should be heeded if one wants to make disciples who understand and navigate life well based on the whole counsel of our God and our savior.

Introduction

Welcome!

Dear pastor, unless I miss my guess, you sometimes feel overwhelmed by the responsibility you bear to shepherd your flock. You know the Holy Spirit has placed you there (Acts 20:28; cf. 1 Pet 5:2), but you wonder about the immaturity and struggles you see all around you. If you're honest, you know well your own weaknesses and inadequacies. It doesn't help that you know Scripture says you will give account for the souls under your charge (Heb 13:17). Even if you normally feel confident, this realization alone can sometimes shake your confidence.

This book is particularly geared for pastors. However, if you're a youth leader, a small group leader, a one-to-one discipler, a parent, or you're wondering how you can be more effective at discipling other Christians, this book is for you. Even if you haven't been called to pastoral ministry, if you are a disciple of Jesus Christ then you are called to help make and mature other disciples. Of course, you cannot change a person's heart; you cannot sanctify a person. That is the Holy Spirit's work in the lives of those who have trusted in Jesus Christ (1 Pet 1:2). But regardless of your role or title, Christian, you are a discipler. There is nothing that is going to make that task easy; walking alongside a fellow Christian is never easy.

Pastor, you are called to your church "for the equipping of the saints for the work of service, to the building up of the body of Christ" (Eph 4:12).[1] Parents, you are called to raise your children "in the discipline and instruction of the Lord" (Eph 6:4). And, if you are neither, you are still one of those saints being equipped to engage in the ministry of the church which is to make and mature disciples (Matt 28:18–20). There is no one technique that will solve the difficulty or guarantee the outcomes for which every discipler prays. Like I said, nothing makes disciple-making and disciple-maturing easy. This book isn't about a specific technique; it's about seeking wisdom in discipleship.

Now, I recognize that there are a good number of excellent books about discipleship available. However, my goal in writing this book is to focus on a particular part of the Bible that exists intentionally for the spiritual maturation of God's people. In short, Old Testament wisdom literature exists for the spiritual formation of God's people.

A Few Definitions

At this point, I've already used several terms that probably should be defined, just so we're all on the same page. Let me define for you what we mean by "Discipleship," "Wisdom," "Fear of the LORD," and "Old Testament Wisdom Literature."

Discipleship. In Matthew 28:18–20, the Lord Jesus Christ commissioned His disciples as apostles to make disciples, baptizing them in the name of the Triune God and then teaching these new disciples to obey what Christ taught. He backed up this commission with His authority (28:18) and with His promised presence (28:20). In this context, "making disciples" is understood to first include bringing the lost to faith in Jesus Christ. In other words, *genuine saving faith sets one in the category of disciple.* However, it is not enough to make converts without fulfilling the rest of Jesus' command to teach disciples to heed and obey Jesus' commands. Along with the positional sanctification that happens when a person believes in Jesus Christ (Acts 20:32; 26:18; 1 Cor 1:2, 30; 6:11; Heb 10:10, 14, 29), believers must work out the reality of their own salvation, about which Philippians 2:12–13 states, "Work out your own salvation with fear and trembling; for it is God who is at work in you, both to desire and to work for *His* good pleasure" (Phil 2:12–13). This is known as progressive sanctification. This sanctification entails growing in the likeness of Christ and in God-pleasing obedience (Rom 6:19, 22;

1 Thess 4:4, 7; 2 Tim 2:21; Heb 12:14). In this way, believers continue to progress in their sanctification, anticipating the eternal state of complete sanctification (1 Thess 5:23). In other words, disciples walk the road of discipleship as they become more like Jesus Christ. Discipleship is understood here as the process of progressive sanctification and not just the "making of disciples" that happens when someone leads a lost person to Christ.

Wisdom / Wise. Since Wisdom and the Fear of the LORD are so closely connected in Scripture, we ought to define them together. Wisdom begins with the fear of the LORD (Prov 1:7; 9:10; 15:33; Eccl 3:14; 5:7; 8:12–13; 12:13).[2] In fact, Job 28:28 declares that the fear of the LORD "is wisdom." Biblical wisdom starts with a relationship with God (Prov 2:5). Fear of God involves trusting and submitting to Him (Prov 3:5–7; 8:13; 14:26–27; 23:17; 29:25); it submits itself to the way God made creation to operate, physically and spiritually. "The Fear of the LORD" is hard to define because at times God told His people to not be afraid (Exod 20:20; Dan 10:19; Rev 1:17), yet at other times commended them for being overwhelmed by His presence (Deut 5:22–29; Matt 10:28). By fearing the LORD, we mean that our awareness of God's power, authority, holiness, and grace all combine to move us to worship, submit to, love, and trust God. Such godly wisdom also recognizes human frailty and ignorance, submitting itself to God's ways even when God's ways make little sense to the best human minds. The fear of God is the beginning, foundation, and essence of biblical wisdom. It leads to greater wisdom and prudence, as the introduction to Proverbs instructs (1:1–6; see also 2:1–11 coupled with the purpose statements in Prov 2:12–22). In other words, the pursuit of wisdom brings a believer into conformity to God's revealed will and way. This pursuit is synonymous with discipleship / progressive sanctification. Or to put it another way, to be discipled is to be led to grow in biblical wisdom. Biblical wisdom is more than mere skills for successful living. Biblical wisdom is a worldview—God is the Creator who designed things to work in a particular way—that leads to a way of living consistent with that worldview. Biblical wisdom is to grow in submission to God which manifests itself as skill in living life well according to God's Word.

Old Testament Wisdom Literature. The debates about wisdom literature—what it is and how to define it—get technical very quickly. Here, it is enough to say that "wisdom literature" is a catch-all designation for those books of the Bible that speak most often about wisdom or subjects common to the idea of living wisely. In the Old Testament, Proverbs, Job, and Ecclesiastes clearly fit this definition. The Song of Songs[3] might seem more difficult to place, but since it addresses the nature of marriage and marital love, a topic that features in Proverbs—and where much wisdom is needed! —there is no reason not to include Song of Songs. There are also some Psalms that are often counted as "Wisdom Psalms." We'll look at a few of those along the way, too. For the most part, though, for space reasons, this book will focus on understanding and using Solomon's book of Proverbs.[4]

Our Plan

Having defined these terms, I'll return to the assertion I made previously: Old Testament wisdom literature exists for the spiritual formation of God's people. With this conviction in mind, the goal will be to accomplish three things with and for you.

First, I want to persuade you to hold the same conviction, that Old Testament wisdom literature is a crucial help for comprehensive discipleship. Pastor, I am praying that you will start reaching for Old Testament wisdom literature in your church's discipleship efforts. Yes, the New Testament has much practical instruction to offer the Church; consider how Paul splits his letters into two parts, doctrine and practice. Yet the New Testament does not say everything there is to say about every area of a believer's life. Just as an example, consider the instruction I mentioned before about parents' responsibility to raise their children in and for the Lord. Yes, the New Testament instructs you *to* do it, but it does not tell you *how* to do it. The Old Testament wisdom literature, especially Proverbs, provides helpful insights on how to do it. Pastor, use the Old Testament wisdom literature both to parent your children and to teach the parents in your church how to disciple their children.

Old Testament wisdom literature applies to many other areas of life, too. The conviction here is that the Old Testament wisdom literature is important, even necessary, for comprehensive discipleship. It is, if nothing else, an incredibly helpful—and inspired! —recourse both for your and others' growth in spiritual maturity. Part One of this book will demonstrate just how important wisdom literature and wisdom concepts are to the rest of Scripture. Even if you already have a discipleship program in which you or your church is invested, Old Testament wisdom literature can absolutely enhance it.

In Part Two, I want to help you in your reading of and interpreting wisdom literature. If you've picked up this book, you have likely already studied hermeneutics and theology and covered at least the basics of wisdom literature. It is, however, easy to let your wisdom literature theology and hermeneutical tools get rusty. The goal here will be to provide a whetstone to hone those edges. If you are not a pastor, some of this might be new to you. That's good! Put these tools in your belt and use the wisdom literature in your own discipleship ministries.

In Part Three, I seek to provide some help with applying wisdom literature. We will look at various discipleship topics that Old Testament wisdom literature covers. The discussions in Part Three could be used to help frame Bible studies, sermon series, one-to-one discipleship opportunities, and counseling situations. I will also provide some further suggestions for use of the wisdom literature.

A Word about Jesus, Wisdom, and the Gospel

In current literature about wisdom and wisdom literature, it is common to find discussions about "Wisdom Christology" and instructions on how to preach Christ from the Old Testament wisdom literature. This book is not the place to wade into the debates surrounding both of those discussions. There is no question that Jesus Christ is the Wise One par excellence (Matt 12:42; Luke 11:31) and that Christ crucified is the wisdom of God (1 Cor 1:24). In Him "are hidden all the treasures of wisdom and knowledge" (Col 2:3). So, we cannot talk about being wise without talking about our relationship with Jesus Christ. The wisdom we're going to talk about here from the wisdom literature is for God's people who, under the new covenant, are God's children through faith in the crucified and resurrected Lord Jesus Christ. The Gospel and the indwelling work of the Holy Spirit make it possible for God's people to use Old Testament wisdom literature to grow spiritually.

One Last Thing Before We Get Started

Pastors, do you want to see the members of your congregation grow in spiritual maturity? Are you eager to see marriages strengthened, with husbands leading and nurturing their families and wives submitting joyfully to their husbands? Do you want to see children grow up to embrace the faith as ready, able, and active church members? Do you want to lead singles who are pure and devoted in their singleness to Jesus? Do you want the resources to counsel your congregants through difficult times and out of sinful habits? Do you want your church to grow in Christlikeness and have genuine testimonies to the life-changing power of the Gospel? I assume you do. While this book won't answer every issue, it aims to point you to an important part of the answer. Through these often-overlooked Old Testament books, wisdom still shouts!

Part 1

The Biblical Value of Old Testament Wisdom Literature

CHAPTER 1

Lady Wisdom's Call: What Old Testament Wisdom Has to Say about Itself

Why should you make a special effort to include Proverbs, much less books like Job, Ecclesiastes, or Song of Songs, in your discipleship planning? In this and the next three chapters, we will seek to answer this question by looking at what Old Testament wisdom literature has to say about itself.

What's It All For?

What is the purpose of wisdom literature? And specifically, what is the purpose of Proverbs? Proverbs 1:2–6 answers that in a series of "to" statements:

> [2] To know wisdom and instruction,
> To discern the sayings of understanding,

[3] To receive instruction in wise behavior,
Righteousness, justice and equity;
[4] To give prudence to the naive,
To the youth knowledge and discretion,
[5] A wise man will hear and increase in learning,
And a man of understanding will acquire wise counsel,
[6] To understand a proverb and a figure,
The words of the wise and their riddles.

The purpose of Proverbs is to provide wisdom and instruction (1:2). Proverbs teaches wise behavior (1:3); "wise behavior" is fleshed out in the parallel line[5] as "righteousness, justice and equity." One of the purposes of Proverbs is to teach God's people how to do the right things and make right decisions. The book of Proverbs provides "prudence," "knowledge," and "discretion" to the unwise. Certainly, those three words overlap in meaning, yet the overlap provides comprehensiveness to this aspect of the purpose of Proverbs. Proverbs provides what is necessary to make the right decisions and go the right way. And, just in case anyone of us is tempted to think we don't need the book of Proverbs, Proverbs makes even the wise wiser and provides guidance (1:5). Lastly, attention to Proverbs will make the reader more capable of understanding difficult but important things (1:6).

With this as the purpose of Proverbs, doesn't it make sense that this book is intended to be used for the development of God's people? Surely, every pastor wants to see their congregation grow in these ways.

Father Knows Best

A second way that Proverbs encourages and even commands us to take the book seriously is through the "my son" language found throughout this book. In Proverbs 1:8, Solomon addresses his reader as "my son," calling upon him to:

> Hear, my son, your father's instruction
> And do not forsake your mother's teaching.

Proverbs is the content of a wise father and mother's teaching. Pastor, if you are a father, you may expect your children to listen to you, even if it is just to consider advice. In your church, you may expect, or at least hope, your congregants will listen to what you have to say.

Well, we have a book of the Bible, inspired by the Holy Spirit, which calls upon its readers in the terms of a foolish child to listen and obey. This "my son" or "sons" language is found throughout the book of Proverbs (2:1–5; 3:1, 11, 21; 4:1–6, 10–11, 20–21; 5:1, 7, 20; 6:1, 3, 20–21; 7:1–4, 24; 8:32; 19:27; 23:15, 19, 26; 24:13, 21; 27:11; 31:2; cf. Eccl 12:12). In other words, the "my son" or "sons" language of Proverbs calls upon us, as readers, to sit down in the seat of the son and listen to our Father. That means we ought to give Proverbs our undivided attention.

Can You Hear Her Shouting?

You know that person who always has something to share? The individual who has something to contribute to every discussion and who never hesitates to interject? Maybe it's a family member or someone in your congregation; you might even feel tempted to discreetly turn the other way to make a hasty—but still dignified and sanctified! —retreat.

Well, God's wisdom is that person. Her name is Lady Wisdom. At least that's what she often gets called. And she is found everywhere. She is in the streets, in the market, and at the entrance to the city (Prov 1:20–21). She's on the highest places and the crossroads, the most conspicuous places (8:1–3). She even multiplies her call through her many servants (9:1–5). Pastor, for your family and congregation, you are one of her servants! And she is particularly trying to get the attention of the simple, fool, and irreverent (1:22; 8:5). She calls to the one who lacks understanding (9:4).

Doesn't that describe so much of what you do as a pastor? You call to the lost to turn to Christ and away from their path of death. You call to believers to grow through the knowledge of Christ out of their worldly immaturity.

And if you're honest, you certainly still have growing to do yourself. Lady Wisdom is still shouting to you!

What does Lady Wisdom have to offer? One can gain correction, the spirit of wisdom, and counsel (1:23, 25). She offers wisdom, prudence, noble and right things, truth, and righteousness (8:5–7). She provides to the one lacking understanding (9:4) "the way of understanding" (9:5).

In case it isn't clear, Lady Wisdom is the personification of God's wisdom (8:23–31).[6] This means that God is the One[7] calling to everyone to come to Him and learn the way of wise living. Doesn't that make you want to use Proverbs and the other wisdom books in your discipleship ministries?

It's Worth Something

Everyone loves a good treasure hunt story. The brilliant, maybe reluctant but still brave hero solves the riddle in the ancient tomb or temple to find the long-lost key to an incredible mystery. We eat it up. We value treasure. Gold, silver, and jewels have been the shiny objects at the end of every pirate story's rainbow.

Proverbs insists that God's wisdom is *more* valuable than all the gold, silver, and jewels we can imagine (3:14–15; 8:18–19; 16:16). In Job 28:12–20, the narrator[8] makes the point that wisdom is harder to find than material riches and cannot be purchased for any sum.

Proverbs 2:4–5 tells us that seeking wisdom as a treasure will lead to understanding the fear of the LORD and the knowledge of God Himself. It does so because God is the one who responds to the wisdom-seeker (2:6–8):

> [6]For the LORD gives wisdom;
> From His mouth come knowledge and understanding.
> [7]He stores up sound wisdom for the upright;
> He is a shield to those who walk in integrity,
> [8]Guarding the paths of justice,
> And He preserves the way of His godly ones.

Wisdom is available to the one who seeks it. But the challenge here is to make sure that we desire it. It is a treasure because it leads to knowing God more fully and walking His path.[9] More than just saying that wisdom is available to seekers, we are saying that wisdom is *worth* seeking. And we pursue it, in part, through investigating and digesting the wisdom literature.

Don't Make Me Come Down There

There is suggestion and there is command. It is important to know the difference, whether you are on the issuing end or the receiving end. Sometimes Proverbs is treated as more of a book of suggestions than one of commands. To be sure, Proverbs does not major on imperatives, such as we find in the Law or the New Testament exhortations. That does not mean, though, that Proverbs does not confront us authoritatively.

One way that Old Testament wisdom literature testifies to its own value is through the authoritative tone it takes. The foundation of wisdom, after all, is the fear of the LORD (Prov 1:7; 3:6–7; 8:13; 9:10; 15:33; 16:6; Job 28:28; Eccl 3:14; 5:7; 8:12–13; 12:13); God is the Creator (3:19, 20; 8:22–31); and Lady Wisdom promises judgment to fools (1:29).

The book of Proverbs repeatedly tells us to heed the instruction being given (1:8; 5:1, 7; 6:20; 7:1–3; 8:10, 32–34; 19:27; 22:17; 23:12, 22, 26). Proverbs instructs its Old Testament readers to keep the Law (13:13; 19:16; 28:4, 7, 9; 29:18; 30:5–6). Proverbs doesn't repeat the Law, nor does it refer to any of the defining historical events surrounding God's people; but Proverbs does teach that one must submit to the LORD, and it ties itself and God's authority together as the same thing. God's authority stands behind the book of Proverbs and the pursuit of wisdom. God expects His wisdom literature to be used!

It Will Make You a Better Teacher

Do you want to be a better teacher and discipler? Surely you can't say no to that! Wisdom literature makes you a better teacher. Consider Proverbs 15:2:

The tongue of the wise makes knowledge acceptable,
But the mouth of fools spouts folly.

Proverbs 16:21–24 repeats the point in different terms:

21The wise in heart will be called understanding,
And sweetness of speech increases persuasiveness.
22Understanding is a fountain of life to one who
has it,
But the discipline of fools is folly.
23The heart of the wise instructs his mouth
And adds persuasiveness to his lips.
24Pleasant words are a honeycomb,
Sweet to the soul and healing to the bones.

Pastor, you are a teacher. You want to see the believers in your charge grow in their Christlikeness. It's the charge God has given you. It surely is a great grief to watch professing believers act foolishly, sometimes even ruining their lives and testimonies. In the two passages we read, Proverbs is teaching us that wisdom helps make wisdom more attractive to others and easier to grasp.

Of course, this is not a guarantee that a certain kind of speech will automatically render every discipleship encounter gratifyingly successful. But doesn't it make you eager to make sure your own way of teaching is biblically wise, both in content *and* delivery? Of course, the New Testament has much to say about how pastors shepherd and how believers admonish each other, but the Old Testament wisdom literature is a concentrated resource for this task of guiding others to fruitful, godly wisdom. The wise make wisdom acceptable and desirable.

What About the Other Wisdom Voices?

Job, Ecclesiastes, and Song of Songs have fewer direct instructions.[10] Yet even these books make it plain that they are intended to be read often and closely heeded. In drawing his conclusions at the end of Ecclesiastes, Solomon again uses the "my son" (12:12) address to call the reader to be warned and to heed. This call invites and expects the reader to pay attention to everything that came before.

Though the book of Job never breaks the fourth wall by addressing the reader directly, God's evaluation of Job's words (38:1–3; 40:1–2; 42:7) causes us to carefully weigh and evaluate the speeches and theology of Job and his friends and Elihu. It draws us into the mystery of wisdom in Job.

We find this encouragement to pursue wisdom in the Song of Songs, too. The repeated calls to "not arouse or awaken love" before the right time (2:7; 3:5; 8:4) challenge us to carefully guard ourselves against undue, untimely sexual desire. On the other hand, the wholehearted approval of the lovers' tryst in 5:1 encourages intimacy for married couples. In this way, the Song of Songs was not written for entertainment purposes; the reader of the Song is encouraged to engage the message of the book wisely.

Wrapping It up

As you can see, the books of Proverbs, Job, and Ecclesiastes are vital for the pursuit of wisdom. We have seen from Proverbs' purpose statement, its repeated call for "sons" to heed, its summary of Lady Wisdom's call, its authoritative tone, and how it helps teachers teach, that wisdom literature is too important to ignore. And that's just the book of Proverbs!

Chapter 2

Wisdom in the Covenant and Court: The Role of Wisdom in Israel's Identity and Monarchy

In chapter 1, we saw what Old Testament wisdom literature says about itself. I hope you can you hear Lady Wisdom shouting to you directly from the pages of these books. In this chapter we'll stretch our legs and get out of the wisdom literature by considering a little of what the Law—including the Pentateuch—and the Old Testament historical narratives—particularly the narratives related to the monarchy—contribute to our appreciation for and apprehension of Old Testament wisdom literature.

The Law: For That Is Your Wisdom

The title of this chapter mentions "covenant" and "identity." Israel was transformed from a large family into a nation when God entered into covenant with His people at Mount Sinai (Exod 19:1–8). In response to their acceptance, God gave them the Law, starting with the Ten Commandments (Exod 20:1–17). So, their identity as a nation was tied directly to their covenant with God and the covenant stipulations which He gave them (i.e., Law).

Why make that point? Well, if the Law is tied to Israel's identity—and it is—and if the Law has anything to do with or say about wisdom then that is strong evidence that wisdom and anything having to do with wisdom—like Old Testament wisdom literature—are close to the heart of Israel's identity. Now it remains to be seen if the Law has anything to do with or say about wisdom.

First, the "fear of the LORD" shows up throughout the Pentateuch as an important attitude for God's people to hold toward Him. When Abraham all but sacrificed Isaac on Mount Moriah at the instruction of God, Abraham demonstrated his fear of God, as God acknowledges (Gen 22:12). The midwives in Egypt did not abort the Hebrew male babies because they feared God (Exod 1:17, 21). Some of Pharaoh's servants "feared the word of the LORD" and heeded Moses' advice prior to a plague (Exod 9:20), but Moses rightly accuses Pharaoh and his other servants of not fearing "the LORD God" even though Pharaoh claimed to understand his sin and asked Moses to appeal to the LORD for relief from a plague (Exod 9:30). The Israelites learned to fear the LORD when they saw the miraculous plagues against

Egypt (Exod 14:31). The men whom Moses was counseled to find to act as judges over the people were to be men who feared God (Exod 18:21). When God appeared to Israel at Sinai, the people were terrified at the display of His power; Moses' response captures the essence of biblical faith in response to God's Person (Exod 20:20): "Moses said to the people, 'Do not be afraid; for God has come in order to test you, and in order that the fear of Him may remain with you, so that you may not sin.'" Curiously, Moses tells the people not to be "afraid" because God is testing them so that the "fear" of the LORD would remain in them.[11] They were not to be terrified, believing that God meant to destroy them, that His display of power and glory was a threat; on the other hand, they were to recognize His authority and power and worship Him as God alone. The right fear of the LORD was important to their relationship with God, just as it is the foundation stone of wisdom.

In Lev 11:44–45, God gave the reason for the food laws: "I am the LORD your God," or, "I am the LORD."[12] In Lev 25:17, God expressly ties the Israelites' treatment of one another to their fear of God. Remembering the identity of their God was important for keeping the Law, just as God's identity and rightly relating to Him as LORD is necessary for wisdom.

We find a particularly clear connection between Law and wisdom in Deuteronomy 4:5–9. In this passage, Moses instructs the people to keep God's Law as they have been taught and specifically tells them, "So keep and do them, for that is your wisdom and your understanding in the sight of the peoples who will hear all these statutes and say, 'Surely this great nation is a wise and understanding people'" (4:6). Moses reminded the second generation of Israel in the wilderness what had happened at Sinai, that God had wanted the people gathered to Him so that they might hear His commands, learning to fear Him (Deut 4:10). When the people had been terrified at Sinai in response to God's self-disclosure at the top of the mountain, God expressed His desire that they would always fear Him (Deut 5:29). Israelite fathers were to teach their children to fear the Lord (Deut 6:2, 24). God commanded the nation of Israel to fear the Lord their God (Deut 10:12, 20).

We also need to realize how many of the Old Testament laws are reflected as subject matter in the wisdom literature: honoring parents (Prov 1:8; 6:20; 30:17; 31:1; cf. Exod 20:12; 21:15, 17; Lev 19:3; Deut 5:16), avoiding adultery at all costs (Prov 2:16–19; 5:1–23; 6:20–35; 7:1–27; 23:26–28; Job 31:9; cf. Exod 20:14; Lev 18:20; 20:10; Deut 5:18), avoiding violence and theft (Prov 1:11–19; 12:6; cf. Exod 20:13, 15) as well as bribery and corruption (Prov 15:27; 17:8, 23; 21:14; 29:4; Job 6:22; Eccl 7:7; cf. Exod 23:8; Deut 10:17; 16:19; 27:25). Oaths and vows are serious (Prov 20:25; 29:24; Eccl 5:4–5; cf. Lev 5:4; Num 30:2–14; Deut 23:21–23). Lying, slander, and false testimony are sin (Prov 6:17; 10:18; 12:19, 22; 16:28; 17:7; 20:19; 21:6; 26:28; 30:10; cf. Exod 20:16; 23:1, 7; Lev 19:16; Deut 5:20; 19:18).

One must demonstrate concern for justice, one's neighbors, and the poor (Prov 3:28–29; 6:29; 11:9, 12; 12:26; 13:23; 14:20–21, 31; 16:29; Job 29:12; 31:9, 16; Eccl 4:4; cf. Exod 20:17; 21:14; 22:21, 25–26; 23:3; Lev 14:21; 19:15; 25:25). One must treat their enemies right (Prov 24:17; 25:21–22; Job 31:29; cf. Exod 23:4). Proverbs 15:8 and Eccl 5:1–7 mention sacrifices and prayer, two features of the Old Testament cultic worship. Job's list of virtues and vices in Job 29–31 is consistent with Old Testament Law and ideas. Finally, though Song of Songs does not have direct commands to the reader, there is a pervasive concern for self-control when sexual expression is inappropriate.

There are many other connections between the Law and wisdom throughout the Old Testament. I challenge you when you read and study the Old Testament to be on the lookout for these many connections.[13] Godly wisdom is close to the heart of Israel's covenant identity.

The Royal Court: By Me Kings Reign

Consider that Solomon wrote or collected most of the book of Proverbs.[14] Although this may seem obvious, we need to stop and think about the implications. Proverbs is clearly tied to the very center of Israel's life and covenants, the Davidic monarchy. Pay attention to the progression in 1 Kings 2–4.

When David was on his deathbed and preparing Solomon to take over rulership of the kingdom, he commands his son to follow God's Law and so enjoy God's favor on his reign, as well as be assured that a descendant of David would sit on the throne in perpetuity (1 Kgs 2:1–4). David was recalling God's promise to him, the covenant He made with David and his house in 2 Sam 7:8–17. David also commanded Solomon to mete out justice to Joab for his rebellious and bloody ways (1 Kgs 2:5). In doing so, David counsels Solomon to act according to his wisdom in dealing deadly justice to Joab (2:6). Similarly, David, appealing to Solomon's wisdom, charges him with dealing appropriately with Shimei who had cursed David when David had been forced to flee Jerusalem from Absalom (2:9). The point here is that David was expecting Solomon to rule and exercise justice with the skill afforded by wisdom. The pressure was on Solomon to make the right decisions in relation to justice.

First Kings 2 records Solomon's obedience to David in dealing with both Joab and Shimei. In the very next chapter Solomon is presented with the opportunity to ask anything he wishes of the LORD (1 Kgs 3:5). Solomon's request is justly famous. He requests of the LORD, instead of long life, riches, and political and military victory (1 Kgs 3:11), the ability and understanding to rule and judge God's people well (3:7–9; cf. 2 Chron 1:10–11). His concern was leading the people to "discern between good and evil" (3:9). This wisdom that he requested had to do with more than just understanding the ways of creation; he wanted to make sure that his leadership of the people was in accord with God's ways. The LORD's response was to give Solomon a "wise and discerning heart" that would be unequaled by anyone else (3:12; cf. 2 Chron 1:12). He also promised Solomon the wealth and long life he had not asked for, so long as he kept God's "statutes and commandments" (3:13–14). Thus, Solomon's wise conduct and leadership was tied to his observance of God's Law, all of which was tied to God's covenant with David regarding his descendants' right to the throne. As noted above, wisdom was not a concern pursued in a corner or unrelated to the overarching purposes of God in relation to Israel and her future.

Immediately after this promise was made, 1 Kings records Solomon's penetrating insight regarding the two prostitutes and the one living child (1 Kgs 3:16–27). The result of this display of practical wisdom was that the entire kingdom marveled at the wisdom God had given him for rulership (3:28). In fact, Solomon became known beyond the confines of the court and even the rest of Israel. He was known far and wide for "wisdom and very great discernment and breadth of mind, like the sand that is on the seashore" (1 Kgs 4:29, 34). Solomon's wisdom was unequaled by the wisest in the courts of other rulers (4:30), and he surpassed other wise men of Israel (4:31). His wisdom expressed itself in more than rulership, too. He was a prodigious composer of proverbs and songs, far more than recorded in Scripture

(4:32). His God-given wisdom also included an encyclopedic knowledge of the natural world, and he "spoke" of these things, suggesting he was a teacher as well (4:33).[15] Even after Solomon failed to follow his own wisdom, by turning from the LORD and worshiping other gods, the author of 1 Kings concludes his record of Solomon's life and reign by mentioning his wisdom (1 Kgs 11:41).

With a foreshadowing of what was and is to come, Isaiah 11:1–3 promises that the coming "shoot . . . from the stem of Jesse," the coming Messiah would possess, by the Spirit of the LORD, "the spirit of wisdom and understanding, the spirit of counsel and strength, the spirit of knowledge and the fear of the LORD." He would carry on the tradition of exercising God-given wisdom of a distinctly supernatural quality in His perfect rulership.[16] You see, Lady Wisdom shouts to kings and leaders so that she makes godly, faithful leadership possible (Prov 8:15–16).

Wrapping It up

The wisdom of Israel's obedience to the Law and the kings' wise leadership were intended to show off the wonder of God's ways, displayed in His Law. God's blessing of the nations through Abraham's blessed family includes His wisdom to live in a way that comports with His rulership. Pastors are certainly not kings and we as New Testament

Christians are not under the Old Testament Law. But I hope you can see from our brief survey of other parts of the Old Testament that wisdom is close to the heart of God's intention to display His glory through His people.

CHAPTER 3

The Word of God and Wisdom:
The Torah Psalms are Wisdom Psalms

Chapter 2 was a whirlwind tour through the Law and the historical books of the Old Testament. I hope it was clear that the Law of Israel was the content of the wisdom of Israel. At the same time, it's important to point out that the Law *required* wisdom to apply it. I find it fascinating that Israel's monarchy, as God intended it to be, was founded on the pursuit of and use of God's wisdom. It was a gift to Solomon, who then recorded that wisdom in the Old Testament wisdom literature. In this way, we possess some of the wisdom of Solomon! And, when God's people navigate life without falling into Solomon's eventual foolishness, we prove to be *wiser* than Solomon. In this chapter we will consider a small slice of the portion of Scripture for which Solomon's father David is best known, the Psalms. As we will see, the Psalms actually point us to wisdom!

The Psalms: The Fear of the LORD
Is the Beginning of Wisdom

I wish I had time to spend with you on the Psalms, but that's a discussion for another day. The depth and richness of the Psalms give voice to worship, lament, thanksgiving, and confidence all toward God Most High. The Psalms provide the script for God's people to use when they need to cry out to Him and worship Him. They guide us in how to relate to Him in real time. But, like I said, that's for another time.

For now, we're considering how the Old Testament teaches us to use wisdom literature. In the list of the types or genres of Psalms you will often find a reference to "Wisdom Psalms." The problem with many of these lists is that they rarely agree with one another. So, we're not going to spend much time on those. To be clear, though, you can find wisdom material and themes all over the book of Psalms. Common wisdom themes include fear of the LORD, choosing the right way of life, the contrast between the ways of the righteous and the wicked, the contrast between humility and pride, the inevitable results of walking either according to righteousness or wickedness, certain rhetorical devices,[17] handling the apparent success of evildoers, and enjoying the gifts of life. For now, we will consider one specific genre: the Torah Psalms. The Torah Psalms—Psalms 1, 19, and 119—are so-called because of their single-minded focus on the Law (Torah) of the Lord. I'm sure you already knew that because you probably use these Psalms to encourage your congregation in their love of and devotion to God's Word. Consider, for instance, Psalm 19:7–9:

> The law of the Lord is perfect, restoring the soul;
> The testimony of the Lord is sure, making wise the simple.
> The precepts of the Lord are right, rejoicing the heart;
> The commandment of the Lord is pure, enlightening the eyes.
> The fear of the Lord is clean, enduring forever;
> The judgments of the Lord are true;
> They are righteous altogether.

I am sure many have memorized Psalm 119:11:

> Your word I have treasured in my heart,
> That I may not sin against You.

Likely you are already quite familiar with these passages. The point I want to make in this chapter, though, is that the Torah Psalms are actually *Wisdom* Psalms, and they firmly connect our understanding of God's Word and Way to wisdom thinking.

Psalm 1: A Study in Contrasts

Psalm 1:1 declares a blessing on the person who avoids the counsel, path, and seat of the wicked, sinners, and scoffers. But that blessing is not only due to *avoiding* the negative path but for making the "Law of the LORD" your delight and constant meditation. In a world awash with media from every direction, it is especially important for disciples to learn to avoid the input of the wicked, the actions of sinners, and the attitudes of scoffers by soaking in the wonder of God's Word.[18] This business of counseling God's people to choose the right input and thus the right path is a common feature of wisdom literature (Prov 1:8–15; 2:1–5, 12–22; 3:1–4; 4:1–7; 5:1–7; etc.).

And, how about that tree and chaff imagery in 1:3–4?[19] That image of a living, healthy, productive tree is a distinct feature of wisdom literature (Prov 3:13–18; 11:30; 13:12; 15:4; Song of Sol 2:3; 7:7–8; 8:5). Particularly in Proverbs, the tree in view is the Tree of Life, offered now spiritually by Lady Wisdom. In other words, wisdom provides the very benefits of the Tree of Life. Here in Psalm 1, the meditated-upon-Torah makes a person into an ever-producing tree.

Finally, 1:4–6 tell us what will happen to the righteous, marked by their devotion to God's Law, and the wicked, marked by their devotion to this world-system. The wicked are mere chaff, the unusable, disposable part of grain, fit only to be blown away. The wicked have no permanent place among God's people and cannot hide among God's people, for the LORD knows the ways of both the righteous and wicked. This comparison and contrast between the way of the righteous and the way of the wicked fits well into wisdom thinking (Prov 4:19; 12:15; 14:12; 15:9; 16:25; 21:8; 30:12).

Psalm 19: Two Witnesses

You have likely studied or read about the two revelations of God's nature and glory: *General Revelation* (coming from creation and God's providence), and *Special Revelation* (the Lord Jesus Christ and God's inspired Word). We find the same two categories of witness in Psalm 19.

First, Psalm 19:1–6 appeals to creation for its testifying value, a theme that resounds both with Genesis and with wisdom literature. Ecclesiastes 12:1 reminds the young, especially, to remember their Creator. Think about Job. For all his righteousness, in his grief Job had forgotten the sovereign power of God to do whatever He wills. Quite simply, Job was thinking and speaking foolishly. He needed to be reminded to fear the LORD, to be wise. Job 38–41 is a record in poetic form of God's challenge-speech to Job. In that speech, God repeatedly appeals to the mysteries, intricacies, and power of the physical creation to overwhelm Job and remind Job who it is that he's been trying to challenge all this time. In Proverbs 3:19–20 and 8:22–31 we find out that wisdom played an integral role in the creation of the world. Thus, Psalm 19:1–6 plays very well with wisdom thought.

But second, and perhaps more helpful to us right now, Psalm 19:7–14 highlights the Law (19:7a), testimony (19:7b), precepts (19:8a), commandment (19:8b), and judgments (19:9b) of the Lord. Yes, Psalm 19 is certainly a Torah Psalm. Yet the overlap here clues us in to the relationship of God's word and wisdom. Verse 9a includes the "fear of the Lord" in the Psalm's list of Torah synonyms. It is not that wisdom equals Torah, but that the fear of the Lord is the beginning of wisdom. In this way, wisdom is tied to God's word and God's identity as the Redeemer (19:14).

Psalm 119: God's Word (and Wisdom!) A to Z

You are probably familiar with Psalm 119 and know that this passage is focused on the value of God's Word. You may even already know that Psalm 119 is an acrostic poem of 22 stanzas. The first word of each of the eight lines of each stanza begins with the same Hebrew letter, in successive order, stanza by stanza. Psalm 119:1–8 begins each line with *aleph*; Psalm 119:9–16 begins each line with *beth*; and so forth. Psalm 119, therefore, provides the A to Z of the value of God's Word.

But, just like Psalms 1 and 19, Psalm 119 signals connection to wisdom motifs. For one, the Psalm includes the concern for the direction of one's way (e.g., 119:1, 3, 5, 9, 15, 26, 29, 32). Take just one example. In Psalm 119:9a, the psalmist asks the question: "How can a young man keep his way pure?" By now you likely recognize that concern with one's way as a wisdom concern. The point right now is the answer the psalmist gives in the same verse: "By keeping it according to Your word." So, wisdom literature teaches us to guard our way by following the path of true wisdom. Psalm 119:9 teaches us to guard our way by heeding God's Word. In fact, Psalm 119:10–11 teach us to hide God's word in our heart; Solomon consistently calls us to hide the wisdom of his inspired teaching in our hearts.

Second, Psalm 119 addresses the fear of God multiple times (119:63, 74, 79, 120). Consider 119:63, for instance:

I am a companion of all those who fear You,
And of those who keep Your precepts.

"Those who fear You" and "those who keep Your precepts" are in parallel. To fear the LORD is to keep His precepts. Fear of the LORD is the beginning of wisdom. So, connect the dots with me: Keeping His precepts is the beginning of wisdom!

Third—and I love this one! —the psalmist asserts boldly that his devotion to God's word renders him "wiser" than his enemies (119:98), gives him "more insight" than his teachers (119:99), and that he understands more than the aged (119:100). God's Word, when we hide it away in our hearts so the Holy Spirit can direct us thereby makes us wiser, wiser than our years and wiser than our education. Psalm 119, then, the most famous ode and tribute to the perfection, power, and worth of God's word, includes wisdom themes and ties wisdom to the Torah.

Okay, What Was the Point Again?

Let me encourage you as I did at the beginning of this chapter: When you read the Psalms, search for wisdom! There is much more that could be said about the connection of the Psalms to wisdom thinking than I have space for here. Yet the Torah Psalms, 1, 19, and 119 absolutely make the point that God's Word points us to wisdom.

Once again, wisdom is not the obscure province of wisdom literature. My goal has been to show you—to *convince* you—that wisdom is woven throughout the Scriptures. I don't just mean that there is wisdom in the Bible. I mean that the Bible, in every portion of it, points us to growth in wisdom. If this is the case, should we not, as pastors and disciplers, open that portion of Scripture that distills wisdom down into explicit instruction? Ought we not take advantage of those books of the Bible the Holy Spirit inspired expressly to form wisdom in God's people?

CHAPTER 4

Wisdom in the New Testament: The Church Still Needs Wisdom

My hope is that the previous three chapters helped to solidify the concept that wisdom and wisdom themes permeate the Old Testament. You really cannot get away from it. And that makes sense since the foundation stone and essence of wisdom, the fear of the LORD, is crucial to the whole of Israel's relationship with his God. Indeed, that was Israel's problem, especially in the end, wasn't it? They stopped fearing God and ran to other idols and the worship of the nations around them.

But you might ask, how can I be so sure that Old Testament wisdom literature really applies today? Unfortunately, sometimes we treat Old Testament wisdom literature as in the same class as the first nine chapters of 1 Chronicles! Here's the question this chapter seeks to answer: How does Old Testament wisdom literature apply to the New Testament and New Testament exhortation? Is it really all that helpful and needed today?

Our study in this chapter is ambitious. We're going to consider Matthew 5–7, James's letter, and the letters of Paul. That's a lot! But we'll help ourselves a bit by looking at each of those portions of Scripture in terms of wisdom and how they interact with Old Testament wisdom literature. Why these specific portions of the New Testament? Well, Matthew 5–7, the "Sermon on the Mount," and the Epistle of James are often called New Testament wisdom literature. They have a distinct flavor, if you look closely, that marks them as wisdom literature. We'll also consider Paul because we're all likely quite familiar with this Apostle. It seems that everyone looks to Paul's inspired letters for theology, especially as it relates to salvation, how our churches should function, and what it means to grow in Christlikeness. So, we obviously need to check in with Paul on this issue. First, though, we stop off on a hillside in Galilee to hear the Master.

The Sermon on the Mount: Jesus the Wisdom Teacher

Jesus is the master-teacher; He drew thousands to hear Him speak with "authority, and not as their scribes" (Matt 7:29). The Sermon on the Mount doesn't mention any miracles at all; the wonder of the Sermon was Jesus' masterful and authoritative teaching. Jesus rightly claimed that He was greater than Solomon (Matt 12:42). His style of teaching blended clear and bold pronouncement with parables and proverbial-type sayings. His parables hid truth from the unworthy (i.e., unbelievers) as much as it revealed truth to believing seekers (Matt 13:10–17). He couched His pronouncements in terms and verbal images that captured peoples' imaginations as much as it challenged their presuppositions and traditions.

The Sermon on the Mount did exactly that. In it, Jesus pronounced blessing (5:3–12) and taught His disciples to live as God-glorifying salt and light (5:13–16). Jesus assured them all that He would not abolish the Law but would fulfill it, meaning that everything He was getting ready to teach them would not undermine the Law but would actually be what the Law was about. To do that, He turned their understanding of the Law ("You have heard that . . .") on its head by getting to the heart of the Law ("But I say to you . . .") (5:21–48). The Master returned religious devotion to private, God-honoring disciplines instead of attention-grabbing show (6:1–18). He cautioned His disciples about their priorities in life, priorities which, if out of place, left them with great anxiety (6:19–34). He warned them about their treatment of each other (7:1–6, 12), and taught them the value of praying (7:7–11). He warned them about false teachers (7:15–20) as He warned them to be careful that they were indeed one of His and not mere pretenders (7:13–14, 21–23). Finally, He insisted that it really was important that they heed His teaching (7:24–27).

But what does all of this have to do with wisdom literature? Well, let's step back to some of those parts of the Sermon. For instance, take those early blessing statements, the Beatitudes as we often call them. Remember the *kinds of things* upon which Jesus pronounced blessing. In the Kingdom, it is better to be poor in spirit, mourning, gentle, hungry for righteousness, merciful, pure, peacemaking, and—even! —persecuted. The Proverbs often declare that one thing is better than another (Prov 12:9; 16:32; 19:1, 22; 21:9, 19; 22:1; 25:7, 24; 27:5, 10), and often the thing that is better is something that seems like a loss or a failure to our world: wisdom compared to riches (3:14; 8:11, 19; 16:16), poor food with love rather than rich food with strife (15:16–17; 17:1), a righteous poverty than unjust wealth (16:8), and humble in spirit (cf. Matt 5:3!) with the lowly than wealthy with the proud (16:19; 28:6). Go ahead, check out those passages in Proverbs and see how our Lord's teaching reflected the wisdom literature. You can hear the echoes. Right?

Or, how about this? In Matthew 5, Jesus addressed sins like anger (Matt 5:21–26; cf. Prov 12:16),[20] lust and adultery (Matt 5:27–32; cf. Prov 2:16),[21] oaths (Matt 5:33–37; cf. Prov 20:25; Eccl 5:4–5), and revenge and enemies (Matt 5:38–48; 7:12; cf. Prov 17:5).[22] Jesus taught His disciples to pray (Matt 6:5–15; 7:7–11; cf. Prov 15:8, 29; 28:9).

He covers the subject of treasure in heaven versus treasure on earth (Matt 6:19–24), a treasure that Proverbs connects to wisdom (Prov 2:1).[23] He taught His disciples not to worry but to pursue the right things (Matt 6:25–34); Proverbs teaches the wise listener to trust the LORD for one's way in life (Prov 3:5–7).[24] Jesus spoke of two ways or paths, one leading to life, the other to destruction (Matt 7:13–14); as we saw earlier, this two-path view of life is a standard feature of wisdom literature.[25] Jesus addressed the result of one's life, the fruit that demonstrates the nature of one's heart (Matt 7:15–20; cf. Prov 4:23).[26] Jesus also warned that some who claim allegiance to Him and put up their ministry activities as evidence will be turned away from Him for not really being one of His own. Proverbs also makes clear that God does not recognize a person on the basis of ministry efforts or activities, declaring that the sacrifice (15:8) and prayer (15:9) of the wicked do nothing to earn God's favor. Finally, Jesus warned His listeners to heed and follow His words, building their lives upon them. Whoever does so is "wise." Whoever fails to do so is foolish and will suffer the consequences (Matt 7:24–27). The Lord's most famous sermon dictates the modus operandi of God's faithful people, and virtually every aspect of the sermon can be related by either form or concept or both to wisdom literature.

The Epistle of James:
If Any Lacks Wisdom . . .

You are most likely familiar with James's concern, "If any of you lacks wisdom . . ." (1:5). That need for wisdom in James needs to be understood in context. Yet clearly James assumed some of his readers could use help in that department. So, you know why we're here. Let's take a look together at how James's whole epistle dovetails with Old Testament wisdom literature.

Right out of the gate, James 1:2–18 addresses the right way to view trials (cf. Job and Ecclesiastes), the source of wisdom as God Himself (cf. Prov 1:7; 2:1–7, etc.), and the creatorship of God (cf. Prov 3:19–20; 8:22–31), all features common to wisdom. James teaches us to pray for wisdom, a prayer that Solomon is famous for praying (1 Kgs 3:3–14). Indeed, as James points us to God in steadfast, faith-fueled prayer, he echoes Solomon's teaching in Proverbs that the wisdom learner pursues God's way, which is diametrically opposed to the way of evil. James 1:19–20 urges us to be slow to speak and slow to be angry while being quick to hear (cf. Prov 10:19).[27] This matter of controlling our speech is important to James (1:26; 3:1–12). James is also concerned with the sin of partiality (2:1–9), a problem that Solomon addresses in Proverbs (18:5; 24:23; 28:21). James 4:13–17 cautions us to not be too sure of the future, making plans without carefully considering the fact that God is sovereign over every plan (Prov 16:3, 9, 33; 19:21; 27:1; Eccl 3:1–8, 11). Indeed, James's judgment that our life is a vapor should remind you of the brevity of life noted in Ecclesiastes. James is also concerned about care for the poor and lowest (1:27; 2:15–16; 5:1–6), a concern that certainly informs the wise living advocated by Old Testament wisdom literature (Prov 13:23).[28]

If you are like most other pastors, you like James's epistle because it is so practical. Go ahead, read it again with wisdom eyes and see how well Old Testament wisdom literature can help you build on the practicality of James's famous letter.

Pauline Epistles: Whatever Was Written . . .

In Romans 15:4, Paul writes, "For whatever was written in earlier times was written for our instruction, so that through perseverance and the encouragement of the Scriptures we might have hope." Although Paul quotes here from the Psalms, his "whatever" indicates that he has in mind more than just that Psalm. In other words, Paul supports his use of the Old Testament by stating that it was all written to instruct.

Second Timothy 3:15 is perhaps even more helpful here than Romans 15:4. Paul refers to the "sacred writings," which we now call the Old Testament. He says that they are able to teach or make wise unto salvation. In other words, the Old Testament writings can grant a wisdom that directs a person to salvation by faith in Christ Jesus. Then, Paul states that "all Scripture" is breathed out by God. Certainly, Paul has no problem including Old Testament wisdom literature. But not only is "all Scripture" inspired by God, it is profitable for something, and the list of uses are all purposes and concerns of biblical wisdom: "teaching, reproof, correction, and training in righteousness." The Scriptures lead one to the wisdom of salvation, and they are also useful to lead one to the maturity that comes from wisdom's activities.

And, just like Jesus Christ and James, Paul's hortatory teaching reflects Old Testament wisdom. Paul speaks often of moral purity (Rom 13:13; 1 Cor 5:1; 6:13, 18–20; 2 Cor 12:21; Gal 5:19; Eph 5:3; Col 3:5; 1 Thess 4:3), a concern dear to the heart of Israel's ancient wisdom writers (Prov 5–7; Job 31:9–11). Paul is concerned with the need to work to support oneself (1 Thess 4:11; 2 Thess 3:10), a concern mirrored in Old Testament wisdom literature (Prov 6:6, 9; 13:4; 26:13–16; cf. Eccl 5:12). Paul addresses the danger of anger (Eph 4:26–27, 31), an issue often addressed in Proverbs (12:16; 14:29; 15:1; 16:32; etc.). Paul mentions covetousness a number of times (Rom 1:29; 7:7–8; 13:9; 1 Cor 5:10–11; 6:10; Eph 4:19; 5:3, 5; Col 3:5; 1 Tim 6:3–10); Ecclesiastes observes the basic discontentment that follows a life pursuing pleasure (1:8; 4:8; 5:10; 6:7). These are just a few examples. We could keep going, but you get the idea.

So, Tell Me Again, Why Old Testament Wisdom Literature?

It might be tempting to argue that, with the Sermon on the Mount, James's practical epistle, and Paul's instruction in Christlikeness, the New Testament has plenty of hortatory material of its own. This is surely true! There's a reason we spend months preaching and teaching through short New Testament epistles. Yet may I suggest another reason to add Old Testament wisdom literature to your handling of, for example, Paul's exhortations?

Wisdom literature can fill out and inform many of Paul's—and other New Testament writings'—ethical instructions. For example, Paul instructs us fathers to raise our children for the Lord, without causing frustration in them (Eph 6:4; Col 3:21), but he doesn't tell us *how* to do that. Proverbs is a father's instruction to a son or sons, and we can read it profitably because we know we need help (Prov 1:8; 3:1; 4:10, 20; 5:1; 6:20; 13:24; 19:18, 27; 22:15; 23:13). Likewise, Paul instructs children to obey and honor parents (Eph 6:1–3; Col 3:20); again, Proverbs teaches them how to respond (Prov 1:8; 2:1; 3:1; 5:1; 6:20; 7:1; 13:1, 18;

15:5, 32; 19:20, 27). These are just two examples. Chapters 7 and 8 will go further with this. On that note, be sure to check out Appendix A at the end of this book for a fairly comprehensive treatment of New Testament discipleship topics and Old Testament wisdom literature helps.

Because the New Testament is primarily concerned with the outworking of God's redemptive promises fulfilled in Jesus Christ, when the New Testament quotes from the Old Testament it primarily does so from those passages that pointed forward or connected Christ to the progress of God's revelation of Himself. In other words, the New Testament does not quote very often from Old Testament wisdom literature (although we do find many echoes and textual allusions). This admission may seem to undermine my premise, that churches like yours and mine should actively use Old Testament wisdom literature. However, I hope this chapter has demonstrated that we always need wisdom, and the New Testament is intricately connected to the Old Testament on this topic. Remember, biblical wisdom is a worldview that leads to actions consistent with that worldview. The Old Testament wisdom literature fills in and underlies the New Testament instruction in that worldview—fear the LORD! —and how to live out that worldview. Finally, there is a rhetorical and mnemonic power to the Old Testament wisdom literature that can grab us and come to mind in the moment of decision if we've hidden it in our hearts. If nothing else, the simple observation that there is more of the Old Testament wisdom literature and that it covers more of the decisions and frustrations of life than does the New Testament wisdom literature should encourage pastors to make more consistent use of Old Testament wisdom literature in their discipleship ministries.

Part 2

Reading
Old Testament
Wisdom Literature

CHAPTER 5

Background and Theology of Wisdom Literature: What Was the Point?

A re you convinced to plug Old Testament wisdom literature into your church's discipleship efforts? I really hope and pray so. I'm going to assume you are still with me since you're still reading this. At this point, I want to help you sharpen your skills with Old Testament wisdom literature.

This chapter will provide very brief handbook type overviews of the canonical wisdom literature books. For each book we'll talk about the author, date, and original audience, as much as can be known. We'll also consider the original purpose and present-day applications of each book.

Proverbs:
To the Naïve, the Youth, and the Wise

The book of Proverbs names Solomon (1:1; 10:1), the men of Hezekiah, who collected more of Solomon's sayings (25:1), Agur (30:1), and King Lemuel (31:1) as the authors of the content of the book. The fact that the canonical book of Proverbs is a compilation—and the compiler is unknown—makes it impossible to know the date of the final edition of the book. However, as Solomon was the principal author, the material of Proverbs was likely written and began to be collected during Solomon's reign. It was concluded at least as late as Hezekiah's reign. This makes the audience of the completed book those Israelites who lived during or after Hezekiah's reign, during the divided kingdom and indeed after the northern tribes of Israel were taken into exile by the Assyrian army.

According to the first seven verses, Solomon wrote Proverbs to instill in the naïve, the youth, and even the wise the wisdom, insight, prudence, and knowledge to navigate life, and the founding truth that wisdom is the fear of the LORD. Throughout the book, the young man, often in the early chapters addressed as "my son" or, alternately, in a group as "my sons," is challenged to observe or listen to his or their father's observations of and instructions about life and how life is supposed to go. Israel had the Torah; they knew what God expected of them. But the Proverbs gave practical guidance in how to carry out the instructions of the Pentateuch. Where the Covenant called for love of God, first, and then love of neighbor, the Proverbs often showed how to do this in a practical way, especially regarding how to love one's neighbor.

Proverbs applies just as much today as it did when it was first written and collected. Christians ought to take Proverbs seriously. It is true that many of the situations described in Proverbs are cultural in that they address life in an ancient Middle Eastern, agrarian society. Yet even so, the principles behind the various proverbs are clearly discernable. Jesus Christ is not only the fulfillment of the Law; He is also the fulfillment of God's wisdom (1 Cor 1:24, 30; Col 2:2–3). This is not to say that Jesus is necessarily to be identified directly with wisdom "herself" (Prov 8),[29] but He is, to Christians, God's wisdom. When believers take Proverbs seriously, they are taking Jesus Christ seriously as He perfectly exemplified living wisely. When believers take following Christ seriously, they can look to the Proverbs to see how that looks in practical, everyday life.

Job:
To the Grieving

The book of Job is anonymous. As such, it is difficult to say with any certainty when the book was written, and thus it is difficult to identify the precise audience and setting of the book. It seems that the events of Job take place during the time of the patriarchs: Job serves as the family priest, his wealth is reported in terms similar to Abraham's, mention of the Sabeans and Chaldeans, and Job's lifespan all suggest a date in the time of the patriarchs. It is important to remember that the date of the *setting* of the book and the date of *composition* are not necessarily the same. At best, it can be said that Israel was the audience.

Job was written as a book of wisdom to record the experiences and responses of the man Job who suffered immensely at the hand of Satan as allowed by God. Most of the book comprises the speeches of Job and his three "friends" who accuse him of unrepented sin while Job steadfastly excused and defended himself. In the process, Job demanded, if he could, an audience with God to explain how he was wrongly afflicted. Job and his friends all seem to have the same basic theology: good people are blessed; wicked people are judged. At times, though, Job defended himself by pointing out that life does not always work out so simply, with the wicked prospering and dying peacefully in time while the righteous lose out on life.

A high point of the book's considerations comes in Job 28 when the narrator[30] asks and answers the question: where can wisdom be found (Job 28:28)? Clearly, wisdom is not found in the disagreements of Job and the three friends. Elihu and his speeches are the most difficult to interpret.[31]

In the end, God steps in but does not answer Job's challenges directly. Instead, He challenges Job to answer His questions, and if Job can answer them, God will agree with Job that Job is right and can save himself. God then peppers Job with a long list of questions about the nature of physical creation, demonstrating that Job cannot understand even the deep things of creation, much less God's purposes in the heavens. Job repents of his rash and foolish speech, and God accepts him, commanding Job's friends, but not Elihu, to seek Job's prayers and sacrifices on their behalf to be accepted by God again. God ends the story by graciously restoring Job's fortunes, family, and reputation. The book of Job taught Israelites the wisdom of fearing the LORD in spite of trials. People must not assume that everything goes according to plan; misfortune, as seen from the perspective of the sufferer, cannot always be explained away as punishment for evil. The book cautions and challenges God's people to be wise by trusting Him and submitting to Him even when they cannot see or understand why God would do or allow what is happening to them. The book also shows God's grace, even when chiding, toward sufferers and the sometimes-foolish things they say about Him.

In every generation, God's people need to be reminded of the basic fact that the righteous often die young or experience poverty while the obviously wicked settle into prosperity for a good and long life. Job teaches us not to assume we know why God does or allows what He does but that He can be trusted all the time regardless. Job also reminds us not to sinfully complain; lament is appropriate (Job 1:20–22; 2:3, 10; cf. Ps 13), but accusing God of injustice never is (Job 13:15–28; 19:6–13, 21–22; 23:2–8; 34:12; cf. 38:1–3; 40:1–8). Job also prompts Christians to marvel at God's creation and His superintendence of creation. No one can do what God has done, much less understand His full purposes in everything He does. On one hand, Job pulls back the veil a little on the mystery of what God does. Yet on the other hand, it deepens the mystery by teaching God's child not to try to figure out God. Rather, they are to fear, trust, and marvel at Him.

Ecclesiastes: To the Frustrated

Affirming Solomon as the author (Eccl 1:1) sets Ecclesiastes in Solomon's life, sometime after his many experiences of amassing wealth, building magnificent structures, engaging in explorations of wisdom, and building an enormous harem. This puts Ecclesiastes in the short period of the united monarchy and makes the audience the Israelites of the united monarchy and perhaps the royal court; "my son" (12:12) shows Solomon had his own sons in mind.

Ecclesiastes records Solomon's conclusions about life and death and frustration after his pursuits of wisdom, madness, folly, and pleasure. Solomon, by his own testimony, denied himself nothing; yet after his many pursuits, he realizes that it is all futile, or at best temporary and fleeting (Eccl 1:14; 2:11, 16–19; 3:19; 4:16; etc.). It is possible and preferable to read the book as coming from one voice, one human author who could attest to the experience of the unbridled pursuit of every desire (2:1–11) as well as to the defeating nature of life "under the sun" (1:3, 14; 2:11, 17–20, 22; 3:16; 4:3; 5:13).[32] Life under the sun refers to physical life in a physical world subject to the curse of sin. To the attentive reader, Ecclesiastes shows that enjoying one's life is a good thing but that everyone should recognize that life is only temporary, even for the wise and righteous (2:16; 5:18; 6:8; 7:11–25; 8:15; 9:9). Solomon ends with the counsel to remember God and fear Him. In the end, they needed to fear God and view all of life as sovereignly under His control (12:1, 13–14).

Ecclesiastes may be one of the most under-utilized and under-appreciated books in the whole Bible, but it is a valuable book for any generation of God's people.[33] In some ways, Ecclesiastes might actually seem *more* relevant than other books of the Old Testament if it were better understood. Christians today need to understand that Solomon was deliberately looking at life under the sun. Solomon uses the cyclical nature of the generations, creation, and individual human life (1:4–11) to show what he means by "life under the sun." If looked at from that perspective, Ecclesiastes makes good sense and has many warnings to provide to believers, especially those living in affluent cultures where the pursuit of material prosperity, ease, and pleasure can distract from an eternal perspective. Every generation of God's people needs to be reminded and challenged to remember their Creator, to keep in mind that they will answer to Him for how they use this life He has given them. Ecclesiastes is a sobering book. It is a book that can provide sobriety to the church in danger of losing itself in a culture already lost to the pursuit of pleasure.

Song of Solomon: To the Twitterpated

Although scholars perennially debate the authorship of Song of Solomon, many evangelical scholars hold that Solomon himself authored it. In this view, Solomon wrote the book as the ideal, even though he did not live out his own wisdom, a fact certainly in evidence when one considers Solomon's authorship of the Proverbs. The book was likely written during Solomon's reign to the generation of Israelites living then. This was the period of the united monarchy and the golden age of Israel.

Solomon wrote Song of Solomon as a series of movements of one love poem incorporating three predominant voices, a Bride, a Groom, and a Chorus. The book celebrates and advocates for the overall oneness of marriage that includes and is partly expressed by enthusiastic sexual union between a man and woman. It does not seem that there is any overarching narrative of the book. It basically switches back and forth between the two predominant voices of the Groom and Bride, describing their love and desire and longing for one another. Song of Solomon encouraged God's people to fight for their marriages and thus look forward to, engage in, and enjoy the sexual union that God created to exist between a man and woman in the context of marriage. The Song normalizes such love and imparts a holy perspective to the physical one-flesh union.

Christians today need to be firmly committed to the biblical definition of genders and marriage; they need to speak when called upon to proclaim what God has said. But married Christians should also be examples of faithful, passionate marriages that make others around them want to know how their marriages can be so wholehearted. By wholehearted I mean that the couple is eager to be and remain married; they are selfless, happy, and content with each other; and they forgive each other when they sin against each other. Wholehearted marriages are, as already mentioned, faithful and passionate. They are "all in." We need the Song of Solomon to coach and guide us in enjoying our marriages. The Song is not a sex manual. It does, however, encourage and teach Christians, within the confines of their marriage, to explore and enjoy what God has given to married couples. Sadly, today many Christians have become convinced that sex outside the bounds of marriage is not wrong. The Song teaches the unmarried not to awaken sexual desire before it is time (i.e., when they are married!) (2:7; 3:5; 8:4). Let's use the Song as premarital counseling material.

I hope this very brief overview of the Old Testament wisdom literature books helps pull the threads together on how the books may be used in New Testament discipleship. In the next chapter we'll consider the mechanics of interpreting Old Testament wisdom literature.

Chapter 6

Interpreting Wisdom Literature: It Is Possible to Do!

Entire books have been written on how to handle Hebrew poetry, the genre of most of the Old Testament wisdom literature. My goal with this one chapter is to remind you of what you've likely studied before. The annotated bibliography at the end of this book will suggest a few very helpful sources. Yet with that said, I think one or two things here *might* surprise you a bit.

Parallelism:
Why Does He Keep Repeating Himself?

English poetry is marked by rhyme and meter. Not always, of course, but often. Hebrew poetry doesn't work that way. So, let's start with one of the most defining features of Hebrew poetry: parallelism. This is when the two lines of an individual verse (i.e., a single proverb) seem to relate to the same thing in both lines. When you studied hermeneutics and got to Hebrew poetry, you likely read about "types" of parallelism, probably three of them: synonymous, antithetic, and synthetic. *Synonymous* parallelism is when the two lines repeat each other. In *antithetic* parallelism, the two lines make the same point, but the second line makes the point by stating it as a negative. *Synthetic* parallelism became something of a catch-all category for those proverbs where the second line doesn't repeat so much as complete the idea of the first line. Still, although proverbs often work just like this, they often don't. So, more categories were created. By the time you finish reading about all the potential ways of categorizing proverbs you realize that the categories are no longer helpful. Solomon and the other sages and poets and prophets who wrote in Hebrew poetry did not think to themselves, "I'm going to write this in synthetic [or whatever type of] parallelism." And, more importantly, the exercise of categorizing proverbs doesn't help you *understand the point* of individual proverbs.

When you read Hebrew poetry (e.g., Proverbs) look for how the second (or third or fourth) line contributes to the meaning of the first. The second line enhances or emphasizes the meaning of the first line, and it does so in various ways. In other words, the lines are related to each other, and the second line *adds something* to the meaning of the first line. A necessary step to understanding Hebrew poetry is to be able to recognize parallelism, and the key to recognizing parallelism is to note the relationship between lines, without trying to specify types of parallelism. But it is also not enough to recognize parallelism, whether attempting to categorize them or not.

Pastor, when you work at expositing Scripture, it is not helpful to merely correctly state the type of parallel, if such can be defined. Exposition is not a test with correct answers to be memorized. To exposit is to expose the meaning of the text to God's people, the flock over which you have been placed. So, your challenge is to let the parallels elucidate meaning. Ask yourself, "What is the relationship between the lines and what is that relationship doing in the text? How does the second (or third or fourth) contribute to meaning, understanding, and wisdom?" Let's consider a few examples.

> Stolen water is sweet;
> And bread eaten in secret is pleasant. (Prov 9:17)

In Proverbs 9:17, "stolen water" and "bread eaten in secret" are parallel to one another. The word "bread" heightens the image because it represents food, more than mere drink. Also, in this case, both are illicit (i.e., "stolen" and "in secret"). The experience is claimed—as spoken by Woman Folly here in Proverbs 9—to be good (i.e., "sweet" and "pleasant"). Her reiteration of her assertion of pleasure heightens her deceptive guile. Of course, the context of the invitation makes it clear that, at best, the stolen delights are temporary, but they will end in death.

> The generous man will be prosperous,
> And he who waters will himself be watered.
> (Prov 11:25)

The first line of Proverbs 11:25 indicates simply that the generous man will be prosperous. The second line emphasizes such a person's activity, strengthening the image of an actively generous person. Also, the blessing of the second line is heightened with the emphatic "himself."

> By the blessing of the upright a city is exalted,
> But by the mouth of the wicked it is torn down.
> (Prov 11:11)

Proverbs 11:11 clearly contrasts the effects of the upright and the wicked on a city, and the effects of each are what any reader would expect from the Proverbs. However, there is heightening or intensification from the first line to the second. The first, line A, refers generically to "blessing," while line B specifies the "mouth," the speech of the wicked. In line A, the city is exalted or lifted up through the blessing of the upright. In line B, however, wicked speech destroys a city. In completely parallel features, one might expect the effect of wicked speech to be the exact opposite of exaltation: degradation or some other expression of diminution of reputation. However, the effect of wicked speech is ruination for the city. Line B surprises the reader with its stark prognostication about the effect of wicked speech, thus confirming to the reader the evil of speech unguided by the Proverbs.

> A fool's lips bring strife,
> And his mouth calls for blows. (Prov 18:6)

Proverbs 18:6 teaches the outcome of a fool's talk but does so in a picturesque way. Line A states simply that a fool's talk—his "lips"—produces or brings about disputes, a point understood easily enough. A foolish person makes a habit of creating strife wherever he or she goes. However, line B intensifies and particularizes the nature of the strife. Such a foolish person's "mouth" (i.e., speech) is as if it is actively asking to be hit. A fool may, and often does, stir up controversy and disunity within a group, but ultimately it is the fool who is asking to be the recipient of that strife. Also, "blows" goes further than strife. "Strife," by itself is banal, but "blows" makes the nature of the end of the strife specific. In the end, the fool is the one who is most hurt by his speech, and he has no one to blame but himself.

See how taking just a little bit of time with a proverb to observe how the lines interact enhances meaning and vividness? Surely these examples will preach!

Rhetorical Devices:
What's with All the Weird Images?

Another significant feature of Hebrew poetry is its increased use of certain rhetorical devices and imagery. English poetry does the same, but the images in Hebrew poetry will often be different because they are from an ancient Near Eastern (ANE) cultural and societal context. Among the various devices used in Proverbs are narrative,[34] metaphor and simile, anthropomorphisms and zoomorphisms,[35] number formulas,[36] acrostic poems,[37] and "better than" sayings.[38]

Let's focus first on metaphor and simile. The mechanics of recognizing simile and metaphor is fairly straightforward. Maybe you remember from old English literature classes that simile makes a comparison between two things, marking the similarity with "like" or "as." Metaphor is similar to simile, but it makes the connection between two things more concretely, simply stating that one thing "is" another. The power of metaphor lies in the fact that metaphor almost seems to violate reality. For instance: Jesus is a door; God is a rock or a high tower.[39] Literally, Jesus and God are none of those things. But those statements force us, the readers, to reckon and wrestle with the ways that Jesus serves as a door or that God is rocklike or fortress like. The ways in which these things are not true force us to wrestle with the nature of Christ and God. Now, as with our talk about parallelism, it is important to go beyond being able to recognize and differentiate the phenomenon. When we exposit the poetry of Old Testament wisdom literature we must ask and answer the question: what is this simile or metaphor (or any of the rhetorical devices mentioned) *doing* in the passage? To illustrate what I mean, let's consider a few examples again.

> Your poverty will come in <u>like</u> a vagabond
> [Simile]
> And your need <u>like</u> an armed man. [Simile]
> (Prov 6:11)

Proverbs 6:6–11 challenges the lazy reader to observe the qualities of the ant which works diligently when it is time to work. It also challenges the sluggard to get out of bed and get to work; otherwise, Proverbs 6:11 will result. The image of a "vagabond" is not supposed to elicit sympathy; the idea is that of a person who mooches off anyone he can and contributes nothing to family or society. The parallel second line intensifies the simile by comparing the sluggard's unsatisfied need to an armed man, someone who cannot be resisted or overcome. The sluggard's laziness leads to need so deep and distressing that it takes everything and destroys everything.

> In the light of a king's face <u>is</u> life, [Metaphor]
> And his favor is <u>like</u> a cloud with the spring rain.
> [Simile] (Prov 16:15)

The challenge here for us, being from a modern, western context, is that we have not experienced the apparent omnipotence of the ANE king within his own domain. Even in European medieval history kings were often limited by their subject lords or perhaps even by a constitution and parliament. But the ANE king reigned supreme. Thus, a king's pleased smile was a valuable thing to have received. The other feature that is important to note is the importance of the spring rain. To a Middle Eastern, agrarian society the seasonal rains were the difference between life and death, prosperity, or starvation. To western, northern hemisphere readers the deep need for rain does not register. To modern readers with modern irrigation methods, the need for the spring rain is not even a memory. Indeed, at times there are places and periods of drought. Yet even then, this often just means the prices of food climb as it is brought by modern transportation from other, less affected areas. Drought in the modern world does not necessarily signal starvation.[40] But in Israel, drought signaled a slow death by starvation. Thus, a king's gentleness of face (i.e., not clouded by wrath) and his favor is pictured as the very provision of life sustenance.

> A rich man's wealth is his strong city, [Metaphor]
> And like a high wall in his own imagination.
> [Simile] (Prov 18:11)

Again, it is necessary to be aware of the lay of the land for the average person living in an ANE culture. The walls of the city provided safety against enemy attacks. Indeed, the "strong city" in view here is one with high walls, the second line intensifying the apparent security being described. To a rich person, wealth is security, very good security. Yet the second line not only intensifies the metaphor with "high," but also intensifies the implied problem of the first line. Such security is only illusory.

> The terror of a king is <u>like</u> the growling of a
>   lion; [Simile]
> He who provokes him to anger forfeits his own
>   life. (Prov 20:2)

It is one thing to say that a king's wrath should be avoided, but the warning is heightened when the king's wrath is compared to the terror-invoking growl of the lion. For western readers who have only heard lions in the zoo or in videos it is harder to feel the visceral reaction prompted by such a comparison. But a king's wrath could be described in terms of a Rottweiler's angry barking or a mountain lion's scream (for those who live in mountainous areas). In these terms, the feeling of the proverbial warning has more teeth.

I think you get the idea about metaphor and simile. They really help to bring the point of a proverb to life. Go ahead, read Proverbs again and take your sharpened understanding of parallelism, metaphor, and simile with you. Go digging; see what you find!

Proverbs: So, What Do Proverbs Do?

Proverbs 1–9 are written as proverbial statements that hang together in contextual units. In other words, you can preach the various sections and chapters of Proverbs 1–9 as contextual units, almost like poetic epistles. These chapters submit well to what we often think of as "expository preaching." However, when we think of proverbs, we tend to think of what we find starting in Proverbs 10, where the individual proverbs so often seem disconnected from each other. I'm going to make the point in chapter 9 that we should not always assume this to be the case, but for now we know how disconnected they can all feel. They can be used in a number of situations, and it is up to the user to rightly judge his or her situation and how well a given proverb, and the wisdom thereof, actually fits. However, merely quoting a proverb, a discrete unit of wisdom literature does not make one wise.

With that in mind, it is possible to say what a proverb does not do. A single proverb cannot capture the sum total of all wisdom on a given subject. Misunderstanding this leads to abusing proverbs to make them into here-and-now promises or universally applicable commands. There is a real danger of misreading the proverbs as hard-and-fast promises of cause-and-effect in the immediate future and in this physical world. The frustration of Job demonstrates that not everything proceeds according to proverbial wisdom as finite people expect it to happen. Surely you have met parents who have claimed the "promise" of Proverbs 22:6 only to either insist their child absolutely will return to the faith based on their faithful upbringing or to question everything they did as parents. Proverbs 22:6 must not be read without the rest of the instruction of Proverbs regarding parenting and personal responsibility.

So, what *does* a proverb do? In Scripture, proverbs capture a basic particle of truth in a memorable format that, when considered *as part of the aggregate whole*, leads one to wisdom in a given area of life. It is important to realize, though, that proverbs are scalpels. They are not swords, and they most certainly are not bludgeons. They must be wielded with the same wisdom they purpose to impart. So, having learned or been reminded of how to handle Old Testament wisdom literature, as pastors or disciplers, let's wield this wisdom *wisely*!

Part 3

Discipleship from Old Testament Wisdom Literature

CHAPTER 7

Discipleship:
How Do You Maintain Your
Most Important Relationships?

Pastor, when you think about discipleship there are likely two basic scenarios that occur to you. First, there is the intentional discipleship that you plan out and—hope to—execute with interested members. Second, there is the ad hoc discipleship that happens when a church member's or member's family life takes a left turn. This latter case might be more often called counseling, but it is nonetheless a form of discipleship. It is a form of discipleship if your goal in counseling is to help the person, couple, or whole family grow in faith and Christlikeness. Should not the goal of our counseling be to see people not just getting through their issues, but also arriving at stronger faith and greater Christlikeness in the end?

In both cases, intentional or ad hoc discipleship, as a pastor your first resource is your Bible. If you've read this far in a book about discipleship from Old Testament wisdom literature, it is likely that you are quite committed to God's Word. To address a specific issue, you search for those Bible passages that best speak to the issue at hand. Of course, there is more than this that goes into discipleship, but to the Bible-teaching pastor this is probably one of the first things you do.

Whether the occasion for discipleship is planned and intentional or is emergency-prompted discipleship, likely the issues fall into one (or more) of the following areas: *spiritual life* (one's relationship with the LORD and dealing with sin), *earthly relationships* (marriage, children, friends, or work), and *character*. Think of any issue you face in the life of a church or ministry to a member, and it will likely fall into one of these areas. This chapter and the next will deal with some of these areas. Here, we'll consider two of the most important relationships that impact every aspect of a Christian's life: relationship with God and relationships in the family.

Spiritual Relationship:
God, Sin & Temptation, Humility

In the introduction we defined what we mean by the fear of the LORD / God: By fearing the LORD, we mean that our awareness of God's power, authority, holiness, and grace all combine to move us to worship, submit to, love, and trust God. Such godly wisdom also recognizes human frailty and ignorance, submitting itself to God's ways even when God's ways make little sense to the best human minds.

I would submit to you, and I doubt you'd disagree, that one of the biggest problems Christians face is an ongoing lack of fear of the LORD. When we lack an ongoing awareness of the LORD's Person, presence, authority, and power, and His infinite awareness of us, we try to live our own way. Even we who are saved can and often do lose sight of God, and we start living life "under the sun" (Eccl 1:2–11) instead of being aware of our Creator (Eccl 12:1–14). Old Testament wisdom literature keeps bringing us back to that fundamental posture toward our Creator. Take note of this: The wise are wise because they fear the LORD (Prov 1:7; 2:5; 9:10; 15:33; cf. Job 28:28). The fear of the LORD keeps God's child away from sin and the consequences of sin (Prov 1:29; 3:7; 8:13; 14:27; 16:6; 23:17). The fear of the LORD provides the promise of security, life, and honor (10:27; 14:26–27; 15:33; 19:23; 22:4). And fear of the LORD provides contentment (15:16).

A life rightly oriented to God's Person and authority will be careful how he or she worships and honors God. The truly wise person, because he fears the LORD, is careful how he honors and approaches the LORD. To honor God is to treat Him with the respect He deserves. The wise person honors God by how he or she uses wealth (Prov 3:9; 14:31).

In regard to how a person approaches God in worship, God loves and hears the prayer of the righteous (15:8, 29).

A life rightly oriented to God's person and authority will honor Him by trusting Him. Proverbs 3:5–6 might be among the most frequently memorized proverbs.

> [5]Trust in the LORD with all your heart
> And do not lean on your own understanding.
> [6]In all your ways acknowledge Him,
> And He will make your paths straight.

Line A of 3:5 commands the wise young man to trust in the LORD wholeheartedly. Line B builds on that command to trust the LORD by differentiating trust in the LORD from trust in one's own ability to comprehend the right way to go. The direction we should go in life is often mysterious, but even when it is not apparently mysterious, we should not trust in our own ability to choose the correct path. The one who trusts in himself is foolish. Proverbs reminds Christians to trust in the LORD (3:5, 26; 14:26; 16:20; 22:19; 28:25; 29:25). It is folly to trust in riches and other earthly fortresses (11:28; 21:22). It is folly to trust in one's own perceptions or abilities (3:5; 21:22; 28:26). God's people have a refuge, shield, and tower in Him (2:7; 14:26, 32; 18:10; 30:5). God's people submit their choices to God and His revealed will and trust that He will bring them to the place He intends for them.

As you seek to disciple the Christians in your care, you will have to help people deal with issues of sin and temptation. You and I deal with it personally, too. Being wise is more than intellectual or theological knowledge. The same fear of the LORD that undergirds wisdom also prompts the God-fearer to hate evil (Prov 8:13). Proverbs counsels God's people to refuse the enticement of sinners who cause others to participate in their sin (1:10; 7:21; 16:29). That enticement may come in the form of flattery (2:16; 7:5, 21; 26:28; 29:5). On the other hand, God's people may be privately tempted through their own envy (3:31; 23:17). Similarly, the temptation comes privately through the discontentment of the eyes (6:25). These warnings from Proverbs match John's warning about the lust of the flesh, lust of the eyes, and the pride of life (1 John 2:16) and add detail to John's warning.

Considering the warning about flattery and the captivation of the eyes, Proverbs has much to say about sexual temptation. Proverbs 5–7 builds up the father's case to his son to beware the temptation offered by the loose woman (also 23:26–28; 29:3; 30:20; cf. Job 31:1, 9–11). She flatters and tempts visually. Christian young ladies need to be likewise warned about the flattery and seductions of unscrupulous men. Of course, today men and women do not need to resort to red-light districts to find these allurements. A private electronic screen can provide the same temptations. The world offers sexual release without the need for the commitment God intended in marriage.

Finally, the many warnings in Proverbs about the consequences of sin, serve as part of God's warning in protecting His people to direct their hearts and lives to fear, trust, and honor Him (5:22; 8:36; 11:31; 13:6, 21–22; etc.). Proverbs addresses many specific sins, and it characterizes the sinner generally. God hates pride, lying, violence, wicked planning, haste to sin, slander, and divisiveness (6:16–18). Immorality is sin (2:16; 5:3–23; 6:20–35; 7:1–27; 23:27). Laziness is sin (6:6, 9; 13:4; 19:24). Temper is sin (14:17, 29; 15:18; 22:24; 29:11, 22). These are just a few of the many topics that Proverbs addresses, but this is already a substantial list of specific sins. Who among us can say we are not convicted about at least one—or many! —of these sins?

Earthly Relationships: Marriage, Sex, Parents & Children

As we saw, we can use Proverbs to disciple young people regarding sex and marriage. We've already seen that Proverbs addresses the dangers of illicit sex, but it also enthusiastically encourages marital sex.[41] Beyond the warnings, Proverbs 5 includes material reminiscent of Song of Solomon. The warnings are dire, but if that is all there were, young men and women would be frustrated. Proverbs 5:15–19 instructs and encourages the young man to experience sexual delight and physical abandon with his covenant wife, even mentioning her breasts as features that will give him great delight. Since Proverbs is aimed at sons the language here is geared toward male desire.[42] However, the principles apply for a young woman also. The female lover-wife of Song of Solomon delights in her beloved's body as well (5:10–16). My point is that it is not enough for churches to teach the evils of sexual sin; the Bible is clear that sex within marriage is not only allowed but encouraged as a great gift from God. May I be frank? We pastors need to stop being afraid to talk about biblically healthy sex. Healthy marriages include good sex.[43]

Of course, marriage is about far more than sex. The covenant relationship God instituted in the Garden of Eden is lived out in the ups and downs of life, as two sinners— even if they are saved—try to figure out how to do life together. Proverbs can be used profitably in pre-marital and marriage counselling. Think about it; the book ends with instruction about marriage. Proverbs 31:10–31 is an acrostic poem teaching a man about the wise wife, the kind of wife whose life mirrors the virtues of Lady Wisdom. Perhaps the women in your churches don't always like it when you preach from Proverbs 31; do so with care and sensitivity. But the point I try to make to women about Proverbs 31 helps (I hope!): Ladies, you feel inadequate when compared to Proverbs 31, but that's just one chapter. Proverbs 1–30 is written to the men! It takes thirty chapters to get us ready for you! So, please don't be threatened by your one chapter, that is actually also written to a man, so he knows what to look for in a wife, presumably because we men are too often tempted to look for a wife based on the wrong criteria (31:30; cf. 11:22).

Now, we don't have the space to properly discuss the many aspects of child-rearing. All I can do here is demonstrate how powerful Proverbs is for discipling children, as godly parents seek to raise their children in the "discipline and instruction of the Lord" (Eph 6:4). The many "my son(s)" statements show how Proverbs is especially geared toward the young (1:8, 10, 15; 2:1; 3:1, 11, 21; 4:1, 3, 10, 20; 5:1, 7, 20; 6:1, 3, 20; 7:1, 24; 8:32; 23:15, 19, 26; 24:13, 21; 27:11; 31:2). Also, Proverbs teaches repeatedly the wisdom of a child who heeds his (or her) parents (10:1; 13:1; 15:20; 17:2, 25; 19:13, 26–27; 23:24; 28:7). Proverbs addresses the need to discipline one's children and what happens when parents fail to discipline their children (3:11–12; 13:1, 24; 19:18, 27; 29:15, 17).

And not only does the book of Proverbs command parents to discipline their children (13:24; 19:18; 22:15; 23:13) and children to listen to and heed their parents' teaching and discipline (13:1, 18; 15:5, 32; 19:20, 27; 23:12), it also provides the *curriculum*, the subject matter that children and young people should be taught. Proverbs covers virtually every area of life. And where Proverbs does not address something, like the griefs and frustrations of life, Job and Ecclesiastes do. Job's description of his ethics, morality, and behavior, flowing from his fear of the LORD, in Job 31, could provide a whole list of life issues and behaviors that should be taught to youth. The fact that Solomon writes to his sons and then instructs them to discipline their sons demonstrates generational wisdom being passed down, especially as Solomon reveals that it was his father who taught him to seek wisdom (4:3–9); that means four generations are mentioned in Proverbs (i.e., David to Solomon to his sons to their eventual children). Think about that. Wouldn't you love to know that your children's children's children will walk with God because you established a pattern of fearing the LORD and godly wisdom in your family? Think about what the families in your church would look like if the parents in your congregation caught—or were caught by—that vision of generational faith and godliness.

The Old Testament wisdom literature has much more to say about our various earthly relationships. I challenge you to search the Old Testament wisdom literature to help you help others navigate their earthly relationships in a wise way.

CHAPTER 8

Discipleship:
What Does God-Honoring
Character Look Like?

Chapter 7 focused on relationships, spiritual and earthly. Here, we'll think about godly character. Of course, sin and temptation, marriage, sex, and child-rearing are all related to character, too. But here we'll dig into a few other character qualities addressed in Proverbs. Then we'll end with a note showing how Proverbs talks about leadership.

Godly Character

Teachability

You know those people in your congregation who just cannot be taught. You can't point to anything specific in their lives that would cause you to pursue church discipline, but you get so frustrated because they are always right and can't be corrected. This is an important area of character to address early in a young or spiritually young Christian. The humble God-fearer is teachable and re-provable (1:8; 3:1; 4:2; 5:13; 6:20, 23; 7:2; 9:9). Fools and scoffers cannot be corrected (9:7–8; 15:12) and only suffer for it (1:25, 30; 5:12; 6:33; 10:17; 12:1; 15:10; 29:1). On the other hand, the wise and understanding can be corrected by a mere word of reproof, rather than heavy discipline (19:25). The student-sage is called to wisely heed reproof and honor God (1:23; 3:9, 11–12; 6:23; 13:18; 15:5, 31–32; 25:12; 29:15).

Contentment

In Chapter 7, we didn't have time to think about the "better than" rhetorical devices. Throughout Proverbs you will find statements that one thing is better than others. In chapter 4, we considered the Beatitudes, Christ's "Bless-ed are the . . ." statements and how they mirror the same value judgments as the "better than" statements in Prov-erbs. The "better than" statements routinely state that a bad thing (from an earthly point of view) is better than a good thing (from an earthly point of view). In other words, *biblical* wisdom turns our world's values on their heads. By remembering what God has called good and blessed, Christians can learn to be content with what God has pro-vided and to find their satisfaction and delight in Christ instead of this world.

Work Ethic and Wealth

Proverbs has much to say about work and the relationship between employer and employee (17:2; 25:13; 27:18; 29:19, 21; 30:10).[44] Proverbs also addresses the subject of need, diligence, and laziness multiple times (10:26; 12:24, 27; 13:4; 15:19; 16:26; 18:9; 19:15, 24; 20:4; 21:5, 25; 22:13, 29; 24:27, 30; 26:13–16; 31:13). Proverbs deals with matters of wealth and debt. Do not be a guarantor for others' debts (6:1; 17:18; 22:26). Sin can lead one to debt (13:7; 20:16; 27:13; 28:8, 22; 29:3). The wise honor God from their wealth before they do anything else (3:9). Wealth is often viewed as a refuge (10:15; 13:8), but it is a poor refuge (18:11). Do not pursue wealth for wealth's sake (22:1; 23:4–5). There is value to saving up for future generations (13:22; 15:6), but the wise are also generous (11:25; 22:9). Material wealth is earthly, but Proverbs has much to say about the pursuit and use of wealth.

Speech

Regarding speech, the Epistle of James teaches us much about the importance of guarding and disciplining our mouths. Proverbs provides the background—and adds so much—to James's instruction.

There is foolish speech (15:2, 14, 28; 24:7). Lady Folly is known for her seductive rhetoric (9:15–17). Foolish speech is characterized as deceitful and perverse or crooked (2:12; 4:24; 6:12, 17; 8:13; 10:18, 31; 12:19, 22; 17:4,

7; 19:28; 21:28; 24:28; 26:23–24, 28). The fool engages in flattery, seduction, and enticement (1:10–14; 2:16; 5:3; 6:24; 7:5, 21; 22:14; 26:28; 28:23; 29:5; 30:20). The fool also engages in slander and gossip (10:18; 11:13; 16:28; 20:19; 25:23; 30:10). Foolish speech is violent (10:6, 11; 12:6; 24:2), careless (6:2), and angry (see the discussion on anger below). Fools talk too much (10:19; 17:28). Finally, fools, being what they are, should never try to quote proverbs (26:7, 9).

And there is wise speech. The LORD is a speaking God whose words are wisdom (2:6). Wisdom herself eschews any and all deceit or abominable talk (8:7–8, 13). The wise father and mother verbally teach their children the wisdom they need to succeed (1:8; 4:5; 5:7; 6:20; 7:24; 31:1, 26). Of course, for the wise to learn wise speech they need to consider all that is said about foolish speech and strive for the opposite. But there are many positive things that can be said about wise speech. Certainly, right speech is wise speech and teaches wisdom wisely (5:2; 10:13, 31–32; 15:2, 7; 16:21, 23; 22:18; 25:15). Wise speech benefits the speaker and those who hear (10:11, 21, 32; 12:6, 18–19; 13:2–3; 14:3; 15:4). Have you ever thought about that? Wisdom will make you a better speaker. Also, the wise are slow to speak; they ponder before they answer (10:19; 15:28; 16:23; 21:23, 28), and they are humble in their speech (27:2). They are concerned about justice for others

(31:8–9). Wise speech is precious (10:20), true (12:17), and righteous (16:13; 23:16).

Self-Control

Wise people learn to be in control of their emotions instead of letting their envies, anger, and fears control them. Indeed, to be able to control one's spirit is a greater accomplishment than conquering a city (16:32), whereas a person with no emotional self-control might as well be a conquered and unprotected city (25:28).

Emotions

In discipling and counseling, it is striking to consider how much emotions are tied up in what people do and decide. The first thing I want to point out is that Proverbs understands grief, sorrow, and what might be termed depression. Proverbs 13:12 observes the effect of unfulfilled desire on the heart:

> Hope deferred makes the heart sick,
> But desire fulfilled is a tree of life.

This verse points out what is often the source of despair: the failure to obtain that for which a person desperately longs. When meeting with a discouraged church member, disciplers do well to determine what the person is longing for, not to attempt to provide what is longed for but to understand what the person is delighting in and if it is the right thing in which to delight.

In counseling, it is important for a pastor to be empathetic. Indeed, the New Testament teaches Christians to "rejoice with those who rejoice, and weep with those who weep" (Rom 12:15). However, it is important to remember that no one can truly know the griefs of another person. Proverbs 14:10 makes this clear:

> The heart knows its own bitterness,
> And a stranger does not share its joy.

Proverbs 14:13 adds:

> Even in laughter the heart may be in pain,
> And the end of joy may be grief.

This is a reminder not to assume that you understand everything someone else is going through. It reminds us not to take someone's outward expressions as necessarily accurate depictions of their heart's struggles.

Proverbs 14:30 notes the effect of the inner life on the health of the body:

> A tranquil heart is life to the body,
> But passion is rottenness to the bones.

This is not the passion of love or the passion of a fulfilling pursuit. This is referring to inner turmoil, to uncontrolled emotions. The person overcome with desire and driven by unsatisfied longing, especially if it is of the jealous or envious type, will suffer (cf. 23:17). The two lines of 14:30 serve together to make that point about the effect of the inner life on the body, but line B advances and intensifies the point by referring to the bones rotting. Yes, the bones are part of the body and so are clearly parallel to "the body" of line A, but the bones are also the framework and physical foundation of the body. The point goes beyond the life of the body to the effect on the very bones of a person (6:34; 27:4; see also 15:13 and 17:22).[45] I am not suggesting that using wisdom literature and teaching a person more about the fear of the LORD will solve a person's emotional struggles. Yet I am saying that biblical wisdom, carefully applied and nuanced, can have therapeutic value.[46]

Anger is certainly related to the envy or passion of Proverbs 14:30, but it is worth an additional note, for Proverbs has much to say about it. Fools are known for and known by their obvious anger (12:16; 14:17, 29 [consider in context with 14:30]; 29:11). An angry person creates strife around himself (15:18; 29:8, 22; 30:33) and will only cause himself great trouble (19:19). On the other hand, the wise stay away from angry people (22:24–25), know how to diffuse tense or potentially angry situations (15:1, 18; 29:8), and are slow to get angry (14:29; 15:18; 16:32; 19:11).

Let me also comment on the subject of fear. Fear clearly applies, as well, to the question of the effect of the inner life on the person's overall well-being. Old Testament wisdom literature tells us that following the wisdom of God leads to a loss of fear (Prov 3:24–25) and contributes to confidence regarding the circumstances of life (31:21). On the other hand, the wicked will suffer what they fear, implying that they have specific fears (10:24). Proverbs 29:25 teaches that it is folly and dangerous to fear people instead of the Lord. In fact, the relief from fear offered by Proverbs comes when one fears the Lord (1:7, 29; 2:5; 3:5–7; 8:13; 9:10; 10:27; 13:13; 14:2, 26–27; 15:16, 33; 16:6; 19:23; 22:4; 23:17; 24:21; 28:14; 29:25; 31:30), instead of others.

Now, let me qualify everything we just considered. I do not mean to suggest that all forms of depression may be warded off merely by reading Proverbs and growing spiritually. There might be real physiological reasons or chemical imbalances a person is struggling with anxiety or depression. Mechanically applying proverbs to a depressed person will likely only add to their guilt and will be less than helpful. However, the wise discipler speaks with wisdom and can help the depressed to grasp any (if there are any) underlying spiritual causes. In all events, growing in wisdom and faith toward the Lord will help with depression and other emotional difficulties.

Leadership

I want to point out something to you. At the beginning of Proverbs, the audience is treated as a son, a youth who needs "knowledge and discretion" (1:4); Solomon has to start by teaching him about the wrong kinds of friends (1:10–16). But by the end of the book, Solomon and others are talking about how kings lead. The final chapter is written to King Lemuel. The book starts with youths and ends with kings. This suggests that Proverbs, if followed by someone in a covenant relationship with God, will coach a person toward leadership. Surely it is a bad idea to call pastors and elders "kings," and even worse for them to think of themselves as such. However, we can gather leadership principles from those instructions to Israelite civil leaders. So, let me list a few of those principles.

Godly leaders lead according to wisdom (Prov 8:15) and seek to do what is right (16:12; 20:8; 25:5). They do take care to speak properly (16:10, 13). They are self-controlled (31:3–4). Leaders seek to lead according to truth—both theological Truth and the truth of a situation (29:14). Wise leaders address sin and sinners appropriately (20:26). Godly leaders are loyal and true (20:28). The right kind of leader brings stability to those he leads (29:4). Godly leaders are qualified to be leaders (30:21–22). Godly leaders are teachable (31:1). Also, everything that has been stated above in the section on child-rearing applies to a leader, too. Remember, the original readers start as youths, simple and naïve (1:1–6), if not worse (1:22), and end, if they will listen to wise instruction, as kings (i.e., leaders).

Also, chapter 7 and the previous sections of this chapter dealt with a Christian's spiritual life, relational life, emotional life, and behavioral life; are these not all areas where churches ought to expect their leaders to be mature? The pastoral qualifications of 1 Timothy 3 and Titus 1 reflect the same kinds of concerns. Paul exhorted Timothy to be an example of a believer in the areas of "speech, conduct, love, faith, and purity" (1 Tim 4:12). So, I hope you can see that Proverbs has much to contribute to the practical maturation of church leadership. And again, even if you are not, nor ever will be, a formal church leader, Proverbs (and all the Old Testament wisdom literature) will make you a better discipler while also giving you the Holy Spirit-inspired material to use in your discipling ministries.

CHAPTER 9

Using Old Testament Wisdom Literature: Now That You Are Convinced

Well, this is where you expect me to give you the secret to using Old Testament wisdom literature. You are, I hope, convinced that you need to re-engage with this often neglected and even more often misunderstood portion of Scripture. And now you're hoping I can finally get around to providing the "how to" portion that everyone expects from discipleship books. But remember, I told you that this is a book about discipleship, but it is not a book about discipleship technique. Forgive me if this seems like a cop-out, but after all this discussion about wisdom and interpreting proverbs, part of the value of Old Testament wisdom literature is having to work with it, meditate upon it, chew it up and digest it. I want to warn you: The following "suggestions" are not magical, nor necessarily even profound. But they do need to be considered.

Personal and Family Use

First, read these books for yourself. Old Testament wisdom literature is not a reference book for counseling wherein you look up an issue and read the advice given. I know you've heard this suggestion before: read a chapter of Proverbs every day and double up for the months that have fewer than thirty-one days. Do this in conjunction with your other Bible reading. You'll end up reading through Proverbs a dozen times in just the first year. Obviously, reading it is not a fix-all for your own lack of wisdom and godliness, but the Holy Spirit cannot use Old Testament wisdom literature in your own life if you have not first "stored up [God's] word in [your] heart" (Ps 119:11). When I was in college, I heard a preacher give the same advice. I had heard it before, but this time I took it seriously. I've read Proverbs a dozen times every year since. After a few reads through, it certainly starts to stick! That's what I want for you. I know you've heard the advice before, but if you're not already doing it, I hope it sticks this time. You won't be able to use Proverbs in your discipling, as I've tried to convince you to do, if it hasn't formed you first.

And use it with your family. My older children are now in the same habit of reading Proverbs through every month. By the time they are my age, Lord willing, they will have read it many more times that I have at this point. Also, once a week our family devotions are about that day's chapter of Proverbs.

We read it through again, each of us taking a section of the chapter. Then we discuss the chapter, and the children ask any questions about anything they didn't understand. Next, they each talk about which verse or set of verses in the chapter stood out to them as especially helpful or needful and why. Finally, together, we pick one of those special proverbs to memorize together as the close of our devotional time. If you're spending time with Proverbs and your family is, too, you will be far better equipped to use it in someone else's life and family. Seriously. You should try this.

Teaching

This suggestion is not necessarily profound, but it is important. Preach the Old Testament wisdom literature! Teach these books!

Doing so will show your congregation or Sunday school class or youth group the relevance of the book. It is also an opportunity to teach your listeners how to handle Proverbs hermeneutically. Pastors, you can also preach sermon series from the book. Appendix A will give you a good place to start for basic topics from wisdom literature with many passages referenced from the wisdom material. You can cover a lot of very practical outworking of the faith from Proverbs. Philippians 2:12 commands believers to "work out their salvation." Proverbs nestles very comfortably into Philippians 2:12's command; here is how to "work out" one's salvation in practical ways, in areas in which believers struggle.

Now, I'll admit the next suggestion about teaching Proverbs is harder. It will challenge you. I've already mentioned the idea of teaching topics from Proverbs, and I firmly believe you can and should do that. Sometimes in a church it is necessary to lay down the biblical expectations about how people are using their mouths. Go ahead; use Proverbs. There's a lot there. But you and I should also consider how to preach and teach from Proverbs in larger contextual blocks. Obviously, Proverbs 1–9 hangs together and each chapter can provide a great sermon text. You can preach through Proverbs 1–9 "expositionally." But once we get to Proverbs 10 and following, we often think that we can *only* handle those chapters topically. Resist that thinking.

One benefit of repeated reading will be to help you see that certain sections of Proverbs hang together loosely by a key word or a repeated concept. Don't ignore those! Preach them! Doing so will enrich your handling of the subject of those proverbs and teach your congregation more about how to approach Proverbs. Let me point you to an example, Proverbs 16. Go ahead and check it out. Look for repeated ideas and themes. And, having observed those repetitions and framing (hint, hint) consider how you might preach a single sermon from Proverbs 16. Again, the Appendix that follows in a few pages is based on the idea that you can absolutely look for topics in Proverbs. But even then, look for *context* for the individual proverbs. And preach those, too.

One final idea for teaching and preaching from Proverbs: use this book for the good of your church's children and youth groups. The book of Proverbs was written for youth, after all. First, train parents how to parent. Parents in your church need help knowing how to fulfill the role God gave them. Israelite parents were expected to teach their children about their God and how to love Him (Deut 6:1–9). New Testament parents are commanded to "bring [their children] up in the discipline and instruction of the Lord" (Eph 6:4). I know you know this, but many of the parents in your congregation may not know how to do that. Fathers in your congregation may not know how to lead their families toward faith in Christ and devotion to God. Proverbs is not everything they need to know about parenting, but shouldn't Proverbs be at least the minimum they know about parenting? It was, after all, written for youth from a father eager to see his son(s) walk wisely in the fear of the LORD.

I say all of this because parents bear the final responsibility for how they parent their children. Nothing frustrated me more as a youth leader than having parents angry—which contempt they often passed on to their teens—because I couldn't reach their teen. It is, after all, the parents' responsibility to train their children in the ways of the Lord. A church can help parents tremendously by being another voice speaking truth to children and teens. This is where an effective youth program can be of great value. It works best, though, if you and the parents are instilling the same spiritual lessons and priorities in the home and in the church. You can take any of the suggestions above, even the one about family devotions, and put together a profitable youth group series. Whatever you do, please don't ignore the value of Proverbs for your youth group. Your youth need it.

Counseling and One-to-One Discipleship

The last section was about corporate teaching. This section takes teaching and brings it to the one-to-one situation, whether planned discipleship or crisis intervention. Because these tend to be far more personal and specific to individuals (or couples) I have fewer suggestions. This is where you'll need wisdom!

That being said, I want to encourage you to use Old Testament wisdom literature in one-to-one discipleship, especially if you are working with an individual regarding a specific area of weakness in his or her life. The chances are better than good that one or multiple Old Testament wisdom books addresses that area of weakness.

Use Old Testament wisdom literature in pre-marital counseling. Proverbs has so much to say about conducting relationships, about finances, and about communication. As you know, financial and communication problems are two of the greatest stresses a married couple will face. Deal with those with them from the Proverbs. Seriously, I believe you'll uncover a lot of things that need to be addressed. It's always amazing to me how a couple will say that they have no trouble communicating with each other (because they are so much in love) only to have Proverbs surface things they'd never considered.

We should also be using Song of Songs in our pre-marital counseling. We should not be afraid of it. It is a beautiful book, enthusiastic and surprisingly complex when it comes to the dynamics of romantic life. I've put a few resources in the Annotated Bibliography that will help strip away some of the stigma and mystery surrounding Song of Songs. We should be using Old Testament wisdom literature in our marriage counseling, too. Just because a couple has been married for years or decades does not mean that they cannot benefit immensely from the wisdom of the wisdom books.

One more thing, we should be using Old Testament wisdom literature in addiction or crisis counseling, as the topics apply. The comments I made in chapter 8 about not presuming too much on our abilities and training applies here. And what I said about not mechanistically applying Old Testament wisdom literature to depression and other emotional issues also applies. There's little worse than foolishly using the unique case of Job to help someone "understand" why something horrible happened to them. And telling a grieving person that what they're going through is just part and parcel of life "under the sun" might earn you a well-deserved punch. Or, at least, they walk out and tell others to never seek you out for help. But nevertheless, we should be reaching for the inspired wisdom literature of both Testaments when we are faced with a person or couple in crisis mode. We know in those moments we are pleading with God for wisdom. It just makes sense to have the wisdom literature on speed dial, at least for your own supply of wisdom if not to apply directly to hurting people.

Finally, always remember the Gospel and the need for grace. Biblical wisdom is founded on a relationship with the Lord. We always bring the Old Testament wisdom literature to bear with heaps and heaps of Gospel-grace. It is not wisdom if we do even an apparently wise thing in our own strength and apart from counting on the magnificent grace of God found in Jesus Christ and His finished cross-work. But if, counting on God's grace and the empowerment of the Holy Spirit, we carefully apply Old Testament wisdom literature, well, that is just a beautiful thing bringing God glory as a marvelous testimony to others about Him.

CHAPTER 10

Conclusion

We made it! Thanks for sticking with me. I appreciate it more than I can say. And I pray that God is glorified by what you read here and, far more importantly, how ministries will be impacted, and people made more like Christ because of your renewed commitment to using the whole counsel of God, including Old Testament wisdom literature.

We've covered a lot of ground. In Part 1, we started with the reasons to use Old Testament wisdom literature. Why should we wrestle with this material anyway?

Because the wisdom literature itself calls you and me to use it. The beautiful wisdom teacher, Lady Wisdom, calls you and me, one and all, to heed her teaching and be shaped by it. The anonymous narrator of Job calls you to avoid the mistake of assuming you understand God, so you don't make the mistake of mechanistically applying the promises of Proverbs and are left to wonder why things don't work out the way they should. The Preacher of Ecclesiastes calls us to honor our Creator while we have time and energy despite the challenges of life "under the sun." Even Song of Songs calls us to ponder the mystery of "the way of a man with a virgin" (cf. Prov 30:19) while teaching the single to carefully avoid arousing desires they cannot yet fulfill. The Psalms connect wisdom and the word of God. The idea is that if you have and heed the latter, you will be growing in the former. All the wisdom material, in one way or another, implicitly or explicitly calls us to pay attention.

Why?

Because Israel's Law and monarchy were concerned with wisdom. The Law, if Israel would heed and obey, would be the source of their wisdom and the heart of their testimony of God before the watching and wondering nations. The heart of the monarchy, how to lead righteously, required wisdom (I Kgs 3:7–9). The nation and its leaders were supposed to exhibit supernatural wisdom. It is no surprise then that Israel's wisest king—until he failed catastrophically—wrote so much of the wisdom literature.

Why?

Because the Church still needs wisdom. Regardless of where you stand on eschatology, the fact is that the Israelite kingdom is currently finished. They failed to be wise! And God is now working through the Church. Christians should be known as wise people, measured and careful in how they conduct themselves and how they speak. Why is it that the church has, in some quarters, such a bad reputation? Could it be that we've forgotten wisdom, too? Shouldn't the church, like Israel should have been, be full of sages? The New Testament calls us to be wise, and teaches us that the Scriptures, all of them, including Old Testament wisdom literature, "are able to make you wise for salvation through faith in Christ Jesus" and are "profitable for teaching, for reproof, for correction, and for training in righteousness, so that the man of God may be complete, equipped for every good work" (2 Tim 3:15, 16–17). In short, the Church still needs Old Testament wisdom literature.

In Part 2, we worked at the "how" of understanding wisdom literature. We looked at some of the basics of the Old Testament wisdom literature, the authorship, timing, and theology. We also delved into how to interpret wisdom literature, particularly the book of Proverbs. You had probably studied much of that before, but I wanted to give you a refresher. I also wanted to help you particularly with handling Hebrew poetic parallelism. We often think of the *synonymous, antithetical,* and *synthetic* categories. These are important, yet the category of parallelism, if such can be defined, doesn't matter nearly as much as understanding the *what* and *why* of the parallel. What is that parallel line doing in relation to the first line and how does that help meaning and emphasis? Don't forget that question when you examine wisdom literature.

In Part 3, we looked at applying or using Old Testament wisdom literature in various topics. We covered everything from our walk with God, to our marriages, to child-rearing, and then to our character. My goal was not to be exhaustive or even comprehensive. It was only representative of some of the larger topics in Old Testament wisdom literature. I wanted you to consider both the breadth and the specificity of the wisdom literature. We also considered some suggestions for using Old Testament wisdom literature. Like I said, and now that you've read chapter 9, I am sure you agree, there was no magic bullet. I'm not apologizing for that. But just like the rest of Scripture, which is God-breathed and able to make us wise unto salvation and is profitable for the formation of godly character, you must pick it up and use it. If anything, all I did was make the point that wisdom literature should be used in many ways, just as you use any other part of Scripture in ministry.

Think about discipleship again. When you plan to disciple someone, you tend to think in terms of Theology, Bible Knowledge, and Character, right? You want them to know God and Christian doctrine. You want them to know the Bible. And you want their character to be formed. That's why discipleship books tend to focus on basic doctrine, basic Bible knowledge, or basic character formation. Old Testament wisdom literature fits all those areas. It teaches us to fear the LORD and trust Him in the good and the bad (Theology). It teaches us to heed and meditate on the Word (Bible

Knowledge). And it absolutely guides our living (Character). Can you see why I want you to add Old Testament wisdom literature to your discipleship quiver? My point is that wisdom literature is so useful and handy for practical ministry, it cannot be ignored.

Work with it. Develop sermon and teaching series from it, both by topic and in contextual blocks. Use it in your counseling and discipleship. Use it for your family. And, above all, use it yourself. Lady Wisdom still shouts!

Appendix A:

Spiritual Growth Topics in the New Testament and Old Testament Wisdom Literature

Type	New Testament Passages	Old Testament Wisdom Passages
Anger/ Violence	Matt 5:22; 2 Cor 12:20; Gal 5:20; Eph 4:26, 31; 6:4; Col 3:8; Titus 1:7; Jas 1:19–20; 4:2	Anger: Prov 1:10–19; 3:31; 4:17; 10:6, 11; 12:16; 13:2; 14:17, 29; 15:1, 18; 16:29, 32; 19:11, 19; 21:7, 14; 22:24–25; 24:2; 26:6; 27:4; 29:8, 11, 22; 30:33
Anxiety/ Worry/ Fear/ Trust/ Reliance	Matt 6:31, 34; 10:19, 26, 28, 31; 13:11; Luke 5:10; 12:5, 7, 11, 22, 25–26, 29; John 14:27; Rom 3:18; Phil 1:14; 4:6; Heb 2:15; 1 Pet 3:14; 5:7; 1 John 4:18; Rev 2:10	Prov 3:5–7; 25; 10:24; 12:25; 16:20; 22:19; 28:25–26; 29:25
Appetites/ Desires/ Lusts (sexual and otherwise)	Matt 5:28; Mark 4:19; Rom 1:24, 27; 6:12; 13:14; 16:18; Gal 5:16–17, 24; Eph 2:3; 4:22; Phil 3:19; Col 3:5; 1 Thess 4:3–8; 1 Tim 5:11; 6:9; 2 Tim 2:22; 4:3; Titus 2:12; 3:3; Jas 1:14–15; 4:2;	Job 31:9–12; Prov 3:15; 6:25; 10:24; 11:23; 12:12; 13:2, 12, 19; 16:26; 18:1; 21:10, 25; 23:2–3, 6; 24:1; 31:4; Eccl 2:10; 6:2, 7, 9; 11:9

Type	New Testament Passages	Old Testament Wisdom Passages
Appetites/ Desires/ Lusts (Cont.)	1 Pet 1:14; 2:11; 4:2–3; 2 Pet 1:4; 2:10, 18; 3:3; 1 John 2:16–17; Jude 1:16, 18	
Avoiding Sin	Matt 4:1–11; 6:13; 26:41; 1 Cor 6:18; 7:5; 10:13–14; Gal 5:16–17; 6:1; 1 Tim 6:11, 20; 2 Tim 2:16; 3:5; Titus 3:9; Heb 12:1–2; James 1:12–18; 1 John 2:15–17	Prov 1:15; 2:12; 3:7, 31; 4:5, 14–15, 24, 27; 5:8; 7:25; 8:13; 9:4, 6, 16; 10:19; 13:14, 19; 14:16, 27; 20:3; 23:17, 19, 26; 26:11; 28:9; 31:3; Eccl 11:10; 12:13–14
Blameless-ness/ Righteous-ness	Matt 5:6, 10; 6:1, 33; Rom 6:19–20; 14:17; 1 Cor 1:8; Eph 1:4; 5:27; Phil 1:10; 2:15; Col 1:22; 1 Thess 2:10; 1 Tim 3:2; 6:1; 2 Tim 2:22; 3:16; Titus 1:6; 2:12; Heb 11:33; 12:11; Jas 1:20; 5:16; 1 Pet 3:14; 2 Pet 3:14; 1 John 2:29; 3:7, 10; Jude 1:24	Job 1:1, 8, 22; 2:3; Prov 1:3; 2:9, 21; 4:18; 9:9; 10:11, 20–21, 31–32; 11:5–6, 9, 18–20; 12:5, 10, 13, 26; 13:5–6, 25; 15:28; 16:13; 18:10; 20:7, 28; 21:3, 12, 15, 21, 26; 24:26; 28:1, 10, 18; 29:6–7, 10; 31:9
Bless/ Blessed/ Blessing	Matt 5:3–11; 11:6; 13:16; 24:46; 25:34; Luke 11:28; 12:37–38, 43; 14:14; John 13:17; 20:29; Acts 20:35; Rom 4:7–9; 12:14; 1 Cor 4:12; 10:16; 14:16;	Job 1:10, 21; 42:12; Prov 3:13, 33; 5:18; 8:32, 34; 10:6–7, 22; 11:11, 26; 16:20; 20:7, 21; 22:9; 24:25; 28:14, 20; 30:11; 31:28; Eccl 10:17; Song of Sol 6:9

Type	New Testament Passages	Old Testament Wisdom Passages
Bless/ Blessed/ Blessing (Cont.)	2 Cor 1:3, 15; 11:31; Gal 3:9, 14; Eph 1:3; Jas 1:12, 25; 3:9–10; 5:11; 1 Pet 1:3; 3:9, 14; 4:14; Rev 1:3; 5:12–13; 7:12; 14:13; 16:15; 19:9; 20:6; 22:7, 14	
Discipline	1 Cor 9:27; 11:32; Eph 6:4; Col 2:5; 1 Tim 4:7–8; 2 Tim 1:7; 3:16–17; Heb 12:5–11; Rev 3:19	Prov 1:23, 25, 30; 3:11–12; 5:12; 6:23; 7:22; 10:17; 12:1; 13:1, 18, 24; 15:5, 10, 12, 31–32; 19:18, 20, 25, 27; 22:15; 23:12–13; 25:12; 29:1, 15; 30:6
Drinking/ Drunkenness	Rom 14:21; Eph 5:18; 1 Tim 3:3, 8; 5:23; Titus 1:7; 2:3	Prov 20:1; 21:17; 23:20, 30–35; 31:4–7; Eccl 2:3; 9:7; 10:19; Song of Sol 1:2, 4; 4:10; 7:9; 8:2
Employment/ Work	Acts 18:3; Eph 4:28; 6:5–9; Col 3:22–4:1; 1 Thess 2:9; 4:11; 2 Thess 3:6–11	Prov 10:2–5, 26; 12:24, 27; 13:4; 15:19; 16:26; 17:2; 18:9; 19:15, 24; 20:4; 21:5, 25; 22:13, 29; 24:27, 30; 25:13; 26:13–16; 27:18; 29:19, 21; 30:10; 31:13; Eccl 1:3; 2:10–11, 18–24; 3:13; 4:4, 6, 8–9; 5:15, 18–19; 6:7

Type	New Testament Passages	Old Testament Wisdom Passages
Friends	Luke 21:16; John 15:13; 1 Cor 15:33; 2 Cor 6:14–18; Jas 4:4	Job 6:14, 27; 12:4; 16:20; 17:5; 19:14, 21; Prov 1:8–14; 13:20; 16:28; 17:9, 17; 18:24; 19:4, 6–7; 22:11; 27:6, 9–10, 14; 28:7, 24; 29:3; Eccl 4:10; Song of Sol 5:16
Finances/ Money	Matt 6:24; 13:22; Luke 16:9–13; 1 Tim 3:3; 6:10; 2 Tim 3:2; Heb 13:5	Prov 3:9; 6:1; 10:15; 11:25; 13:7–8, 22; 15:6; 17:18; 18:11; 20:16; 22:1, 9, 26; 23:4–5; 27:13; 28:8, 22; 29:3
Marriage / Sexual Purity	Matt 5:27–32; 19:9–10; 22:30; Mark 10:11–12; 12:25; Luke 16:18; 20:34–35; Rom 7:2; 1 Cor 6:9–10, 15–20; 7 (whole chapter); Gal 5:19; Eph 5:3–5; 22–33; Col 3:5, 18–19; 1 Tim 3:2, 12; Titus 1:6; Heb 13:4	Job 31:1, 9–12; Prov 2:16–19; 5:1–23; 6:20–35; 7:1–27; 17:15–16; 21:9, 19; 23:26–28; 25:24; 31:10–31; Eccl 2:8; 9:9; Song of Solomon (whole book)
Obedience	John 3:36; Acts 5:29, 32; Rom 1:30; 6:12, 16; 15:18; 16:19; 2 Cor 2:9; 7:15; 9:13; 10:5–6;	Prov 1:8; 3:1, 21; 4:1–2, 4, 13, 21; 5:12–13, 23; 6:20, 23; 7:1–2; 8:32–33;

Type	New Testament Passages	Old Testament Wisdom Passages
Obedience (Cont.)	Eph 6:1, 5; Phil 2:12; Col 3:20, 22; 2 Thess 1:8; 3:14; 2 Tim 3:2; Titus 3:1; Heb 5:9; 13:17; 1 Pet 1:2, 14; 3:1–6; 4:17;	10:8, 17; 13:13; 19:16; 22:18; 28:4, 7; 29:18; Eccl 8:2, 5; 12:13–14
Parenting	Eph 6:4; Col 3:21; 1 Tim 3:4–5; Titus 1:6; (cf. Heb 12:9; Matt 7:9–11; Luke 11:13)	Prov 1:8, 10, 15; 2:1; 3:1, 11, 21; 4:10, 20; 5:1, 7, 20; 6:1, 3, 20; 7:1, 24; 8:32; 10:1; 13:1, 22, 24; 14:26; 15:5, 20; 17:6; 19:18, 26–27; 20:20; 22:6, 15; 23:13–15, 19, 22, 25–26; 24:13, 21; 27:11; 28:24; 29:15, 21; 30:11, 17; 31:1–2, 28; Eccl 12:12
Pride	Mark 7:22; Luke 1:51; Rom 1:30; 11:18; 12:16; 1 Cor 4:6, 18–19; 5:2; 8:1; 13:4; 2 Cor 5:12; 11:18, 30; 2 Tim 3:2, 14; Jas 4:6; 1 Pet 5:5; 2 Pet 2:18; 1 John 2:16; Jude 1:16; Rev 13:5	Job 40:12; Prov 1:22; 3:34; 6:17; 8:13; 9:7–8, 12; 11:2; 13:1, 10; 14:6, 16; 15:12, 25; 16:5, 18–19; 18:12; 19:25, 29; 21:4, 11, 24; 22:10; 24:9; 28:25; 29:23

Type	New Testament Passages	Old Testament Wisdom Passages
Speech	Matt 5:33–37; 12:34–36; John 8:44; Acts 5:3; Rom 16:18; 1 Cor 13:11; Eph 4:24–27, 29, 31–32; 5:3–4, 11–12; Col 3:8–9; 4:6; 1 Tim 4:12; Titus 2:8; Jas 3:1–12; 4:11; 1 John 4:5; Jude 1:16;	Job 2:13; 38:1–2; 40:1–5; 42:1–7; Prov 1:8, 10–14; 2:6, 12, 16; 4:4, 24; 5:2–3, 7; 6:2, 12, 17, 20, 24; 7:5, 21, 24; 8:7–8, 13; 9:15–17; 10:6, 11, 13, 18–20, 31–32; 11:13; 12:6, 17–19, 22; 13:2–3; 14:3; 15:2, 4, 7, 14, 28; 16:13, 21, 23, 28; 17:4, 7, 28; 18:20–21; 19:28; 20:19; 21:23, 28; 22:14, 18; 23:16; 24:2, 7, 28; 25:15, 23; 26:7, 9, 23–24, 28; 27:2; 28:23; 29:5; 30:10, 20; 31:1, 8–9, 26; Eccl 5:1–7; 6:11; 7:21; 9:17; 10:12, 14; 12:10–11
Strife/ Disputes	Luke 22:24; Rom 1:29; 13:13; 1 Cor 1:11; 3:3; 2 Cor 12:20; Gal 5:20; Phil 1:15; 2:14; 1 Tim 6:4; 2 Tim 2:23–24; Titus 3:9; Jas 4:1–2	Prov 6:14, 19; 10:12; 13:10; 15:18; 16:28; 17:1, 14, 19; 18:1, 6, 18; 20:3; 22:10; 25:8–9; 26:17, 21; 28:25; 29:22; 30:33

APPENDIX B:
Recommended Resources

This annotated bibliography is intended to provide just a few helpful sources for using and understanding Old Testament wisdom literature. The list is broken down in matters of Ancient Near East Background, Discipleship, Interpretation, Preaching, and Wisdom Christology. Some of these are items we never covered in the body of this book. They are included for those who want to do more study on relevant topics related to Old Testament wisdom literature.

Ancient Near East Background

Fox, Michael V. "From Amenemope to Proverbs." *Zeitschrift für die Alttestamentliche Wissenschaft* 126, no. 1 (2014): 76–91.

Michael Fox's article is an example of the assumption that Proverbs, or portions of it, are dependent upon existing material from the cultures around Israel. Fox gives great credit to the biblical sage for how he compiled such material, in this case Egyptian wisdom material, but he nonetheless takes the Egyptian material as antecedent to Israelite wisdom literature.

Ruffle, John. "The Teaching of Amenemope and its Connection with the Book of Proverbs." *Tyndale Bulletin* 28 (1977): 29–68.

In contrast to Michael Fox's article (above), John Ruffle addresses and argues against the conclusion that the Israelite material is dependent upon other wisdom material.

Waltke, Bruce K. "The Book of Proverbs and Ancient Wisdom Literature." *Bibliotheca Sacra* 136, no. 543 (July 1979): 221–238.

Bruce Waltke's article concurs with Michael Fox's thesis but addresses the question more broadly than with just one particular passage within Proverbs. These three studies are mentioned to illustrate some of the ongoing debates on how understanding the issues aids in handling Proverbs.

Walton, John H. *Ancient Near Eastern Thought and the Old Testament: Introducing the Conceptual World of the Hebrew Bible*, 2nd ed. Grand Rapids: Baker Academic, 2018.

John Walton's book is a helpful resource that overviews the mindset that drove Ancient Near East culture. The Israelites would have partaken of this mindset and background, and Walton's book is a helpful one-stop-shop of information on this subject.

Discipleship

Brown, William P. *Character in Crisis: A Fresh Approach to the Wisdom Literature of the Old Testament*. Grand Rapids: Eerdmans, 1996.

William Brown seeks to apply Old Testament wisdom literature to the question of character. His emphasis is refreshing since discipleship is certainly concerned with the formation of Christian character. He considers Proverbs, Job, and Ecclesiastes theologically from the question of what they each have to do with the formation of a person's character.

Leman, Derek. *Proverbial Wisdom & Common Sense: A Messianic Jewish Approach to Today's Issues from the Proverbs*. Baltimore: Lederer Messianic Publications, 1999.

Derek Leman's book is something of a devotional guide to using Proverbs in everyday ways. He works through the prologue material (Prov 1–9), considers the rest of Proverbs topically, and then handles Proverbs 30 and 31 as separate discourses. The book is easy to read and can make a useful devotional guide for family devotions.

Yost, Robert A. *Leadership Secrets from the Proverbs: An Examination of Leadership Principles from the Book of Proverbs*. Eugene: Wipf and Stock Publishers, 2013.

Robert Yost's book is a published version of his Ph.D. dissertation, but it is very practical. It could be used with great profit for leading a young pastoral intern or team of pastors in examining and building their character. He especially focuses on matters of the tongue since leaders do much speaking.

Interpretation

Alter, Robert. *The Art of Biblical Poetry*. New York: Basic Books, 2011.

Kugel, James. *The Idea of Biblical Poetry: Parallelism and Its History*. Baltimore: Johns Hopkins University Press, 1998.

Longman, Tremper. *How to Read the Psalms*. Downers Grove: InterVarsity, 1988.

Robert Alter and James Kugel are invaluable for making sense of poetic parallelism. They both provide multiple examples throughout their discussions of parallelism, including some from Proverbs. Tremper Longman's little book on Psalms is included here because Proverbs is written in Hebrew poetry, and Longman's assistance with Psalms is helpful with Proverbs as well.

Longman, Tremper. *The Fear of the Lord Is Wisdom: A Theological Introduction to Wisdom in Israel*. Grand Rapids: Baker Academic, 2017.

This book by Tremper Longman is a helpful primer on the theology of Old Testament wisdom literature. Of the canonical books, Longman covers Proverbs, Job, and Ecclesiastes. The reader should be careful of his conclusions in places, especially regarding Ecclesiastes. However, the book overall is a welcome overview of the theology of wisdom literature.

McGinniss, Mark. *Contributions of Selected Rhetorical Devices to a Biblical Theology of The Song of Songs.* Eugene, OR: Wipf and Stock, 2011.

Mark McGinniss's book is the published version of his Ph.D. dissertation on the Song of Solomon. It is technical reading, but his conclusions are helpful for careful readers. He argues, as here in this project, that the church needs to recover a contextual reading of Song of Solomon and use the book as it was intended to be used. His analysis of the book along specific rhetorical lines helps do that.

Waltke, Bruce K. *The Book of Proverbs, Chapters 1–15.* Grand Rapids: Eerdmans, 2004.

Waltke, Bruce K. *The Book of Proverbs, Chapters 15–31.* Grand Rapids: Eerdmans, 2005.

Bruce Waltke's two volume commentary set is not the only commentary available, but it might be the best available. It can, at times, lean heavily on Hebrew grammar and syntax, but his interpretive conclusions are helpful. Waltke is especially helpful in his analysis of Proverbs along contextual lines. He is good at perceiving proverb groupings and exegeting individual proverbs in line with the group, a point dealt with slightly in this book's chapter 9.

Preaching

Waltke, Bruce K. "Fundamentals for Preaching the Book of Proverbs, Part 1." *Bibliotheca Sacra* 165, no. 657 (January 2008): 3–12.

Waltke, Bruce K. "Fundamentals for Preaching the Book of Proverbs, Part 2." *Bibliotheca Sacra* 165, no. 658 (April 2008): 131–144.

Waltke, Bruce K. "Fundamentals for Preaching the Book of Proverbs, Part 3." *Bibliotheca Sacra* 165, no. 659 (July 2008): 259–267.

Waltke, Bruce K. "Fundamentals for Preaching the Book of Proverbs, Part 4." *Bibliotheca Sacra* 165, no. 660 (October 2008): 387–396.

Bruce Waltke's four-part article series on preaching from Proverbs is helpful, especially since he prefers to preach from proverb groupings, though he does acknowledge the validity of topical or single-proverb messages from Proverbs. He argues that the church needs to be preaching from Proverbs, a point near and dear to the heart of this project. He also acknowledges the difficulty of knowing how to preach from the Proverbs.

Wisdom Christology

Ebert, Daniel J. *Wisdom Christology: How Jesus Becomes God's Wisdom for Us*. Phillipsburg, NJ: P & R, 2011.

Fee, Gordon D. *Pauline Christology: An Exegetical-Theological Study*. Grand Rapids: Baker Academic, 2007.

In these books, Daniel Ebert and Gordon Fee both wade into the muddy waters of the question of Christ's relationship to Old Testament wisdom. They are both conservative in their outlook and can be read with great profit. They arrive at different conclusions, but both conclusions are orthodox. Ebert is willing to grant the reality of a "wisdom Christology," hence his title. Fee argues strongly against the existence of a wisdom Christology, at least within Paul.

About the Author

Scott Corbin received his Bachelor of Science (Physics) and Master of Education (Mathematics) from Bob Jones University. He had planned to pursue a career as a scientist or science and math teacher, yet God used the church where he and his wife, Barbi, were married to lead him toward seminary and vocational ministry. He earned his Master of Divinity and Doctor of Ministry (Biblical Exposition) from Baptist Bible Seminary (Clarks Summit, Pennsylvania). He and his wife Barbi have done just about everything there is to do in a church. He has been in full-time ministry since 2013 and was ordained in 2016 at New Testament Baptist Church. Scott has been the shepherd at Christ Is King Baptist Church in Nedrow, New York since January 2022. He and Barbi have been married for 18 years and have three children, Samuel, Bryce, and Noella.

Endnotes

1   All Scripture quotations are from the New American Standard Bible (1995) unless otherwise indicated.

2   "LORD" is in all capitals to match where English translations use "LORD" to translate the covenant name of God (YHWH/Yahweh/Jehovah).

3   Song of Songs is another title for the Song of Solomon. "Song of Songs" comes directly from the first line of Song of Songs: "The Song of Songs, which is Solomon's."

4   The *Wisdom of Solomon* and the *Wisdom of Ben Sirach* are two non-canonical wisdom books that appear in the literature about wisdom literature, but we're only focusing on the canonical wisdom books.

'

Chapter 1 Notes:

5   We will talk about the importance of understanding the phenomenon of Hebrew parallelism in chapter 6.

6   By "personification," I mean that Lady Wisdom is a *literary* personification of an attribute of God, not a *literal* personification of God or of any member of the Trinity. Some versions of "Wisdom Christology" like to claim this or get close to claiming this, but the Proverbs passages simply cannot bear that much theological weight. Nor is such a theological claim necessary

to make sense of the rhetorical device of anthropomorphizing an attribute of God.

7   By saying that God is calling when Lady Wisdom is calling, I do not mean that God is in any sense female.

8   There is a debate over who is speaking in Job 28. Some think Job is still speaking in Job 28, while others think that Job 28 is a narrator's insertion. The identity of the speaker in Job 28 does not change the point about the value of wisdom.

9   "Path" / "way" is an important wisdom theme in Proverbs, as in the way of the righteous and the way of the wicked.

10 If we included the "Wisdom Psalms," which are admittedly hard to define, we would find even more instruction related to heeding wisdom literature, especially in the Torah Psalms (1; 19; and 119). We'll get to those in chapter 3.

Chapter 2 Notes:

11 "Afraid" and "fear" are two related Hebrew words.

12 For other examples of the same phenomenon, read Lev 18:2, 4–6, 21, 30; 19:3–4, 10, 12, 14, 18, 25, 28, 30–32, 34, 36, 37; 20:7–8, 24; 21:12, 15, 23; 22:2–3, 8–9, 16, 30–33; 23:22, 43; 24:22; 25:17, 38, 55; 26:1–2, 13, 44–45.

13 After all, one of the tactics of wisdom literature is to call the learner to dig for his or her wisdom. To get you started, here are some clues as to where to find just a few others: Deut 34; Josh 1:8; 2 Chron 30:22 (cf. Prov 12:8a); Jer

8:9; Mal 2:1–9. Also, the whole book of Deuteronomy has much to add to this topic.

14 Yes, I take the witness of Prov 1:1; 25:1 very seriously, modern critical scholarship notwithstanding. Solomon wrote most of the book. The only portions Solomon did not write are those portions expressly attributed to other authors.

15 King Hiram of Tyre (1 Kgs 5:7, 12; 2 Chron 2:12) and the Queen of Sheba (1 Kgs 10:1–9; 2 Chron 9:8) were just two foreign monarchs of many who testified to Solomon's wisdom (1 Kgs 10:24; 2 Chron 9:23).

16 Regarding the prophets, there wasn't space in this chapter to examine the prophetic books, but since the prophets engaged in covenant enforcement, the prophets would have been concerned about Israel's defection from godly wisdom.

Chapter 3 Notes:

17 We'll talk about some of those rhetorical devices in chapter 6.

18 Yes, I know that Torah specifically refers to the Law. Actually, "torah" means "instruction" and came to be the technical designation for those books known as the Law. As it relates to the Torah Psalms, I am conflating Torah (Law) and God's Word, though God's Word was certainly not complete as of the writing of the Torah Psalms. The point remains the same. Holding to verbal, plenary inspiration and the progress of Scripture means applying the "instruction" of the Torah Psalms to the whole of Scripture.

19 Technically, this is a simile, introduced, as it is, with "like." Again, we'll talk about poetic devices in chapter 6.

Chapter 4 Notes:

20 See also Prov 14:29; 15:1, 18; 16:32; 19:11, 19; 22:24; 29:8, 22; 30:33.

21 And Prov 5–7; 11:22; 22:14; 23:26–27; 30:20.

22 Keep reading: Prov 24:17; 25:21–22.

23 Also, Prov 7:1; 15:16; 21:20; 23:4–5.

24 Prov 16:3, 9, 33; 22:19.

25 Prov 1:15; 2:8, 12–13, 15; 3:17; 4:11, 14–15, 19, 26; 8:20; 9:6; 12:26, 28.

26 Prov 11:30; 12:12, 14; 18:20.

27 Prov 13:3; 14:17, 29; 15:18; 16:32; 17:27; 18:13; 19:11, 19; 21:23; 25:28; Eccl 5:2–3; 7:8–9.

28 Prov 14:20–21, 31; 17:5; 18:23; 19:4, 7, 17; 21:13; 22:2, 9, 16, 22; 28:3, 15, 27; 29:7, 13–14; 31:20; Job 31:16–21; Eccl 5:8.

Chapter 5 Notes:

29 Some scholars like to argue this, that Lady Wisdom has something to do with the pre-incarnate Christ. This view is

often called "wisdom Christology." This is not the place to go into why I disagree with that position. Check out the recommended resources for a couple of sources to help with this question.

30 There is debate over whether this is Job or the narrator, but the overall point is not materially changed either way.

31 I believe that Elihu is a good character whose speeches prepare the way for God's direct speeches to Job. Elihu bucks the trend of Job's and the friends' theology. This is why God doesn't condemn Elihu's words or make him seek Job's intercessory ministry (Job 42:7–9). But I agree that it can be hard to be sure.

32 You're probably aware of the debates about the authorship and structure of Ecclesiastes. It is common and popular to attribute the book to two authors, neither of whom is Solomon. The "frame narrator" writes chapters 1 and 12 to correct the "flawed" thinking of "Qoheleth," the Preacher, a bitter and frustrated wisdom teacher. Such a view of the book is unnecessary. The admitted "under the sun" perspective provides all the framework we need to understand what Solomon is doing in the book.

33 I have personally led a men's Bible study / discipleship group verse-by-verse through Ecclesiastes. I highly recommend it.

Chapter 6 Notes:

34 Narrative: See Prov 7:6–23. Solomon's observation of a young man being enticed by and then walking away with a

seductive, adulterous wife brings the warnings of Prov 5 and 6 home in a graphic way. We the reader view the scene from the teacher's or wise person's vantage, wanting to shout after the young man, "No, don't go with her!" It moves us to think carefully about our own susceptibilities.

35 Anthropomorphisms and zoomorphisms: Check out Prov 8–9; 20:2; 21:1; 23:5. As you probably know, these are the practice of attributing either human or animal characteristics to a concept (like wisdom as a lady) or person (like God). These are related to simile and metaphor, giving us images of an abstract concept or invisible person to help us grasp the nature of the thing or person thus described.

36 Number formulas: Read Prov 6:16; 30:18, 21, 24, 29. These can be described as X, no X+1 statements. The purpose of these is to draw attention to a list, heighten meaning and understanding, and possibly emphasize the +1 (the last item).

37 Acrostic poems: Look at Prov 31:10–31. The book ends with an acrostic poem about the wise wife, the suitable companion to the man trained by the book of Proverbs. Each verse begins with a successive letter of the Hebrew alphabet. You could think of this as the A-Z of the ideal wife. Acrostic poems draw attention to the completeness of the description being given. Psalm 119, which we looked at in chapter 3, is such an acrostic about the word of God.

38 Consider Prov 8:11, 19; 15:16, 17; 16:8, 19, 32. We talked about these in chapter 4.

39 It is helpful to realize that much of the work of theology is the work of metaphor. Because God is infinite and we are finite, we have no choice—and Scripture does the same

thing—but to talk about God in terms we can understand and that includes verbal images.

40 Written as this is in 2023 after years of news of dreadful droughts and dried up rivers and reservoirs in the U.S., my comments may seem tone deaf. However, the fact that our droughts make for so much news just establishes what I'm saying, that we are not used to it. And, even as food prices do skyrocket, very few of us are actually going hungry.

Chapter 7 Notes:

41 The books of Job (31:1, 9–12) and Ecclesiastes (2:8; 9:9) can contribute a little bit to the subject of sex and marital fidelity. Song of Solomon is a wisdom book about marital union, companionship, and harmony. Song of Solomon also celebrates the sexual union that emblemizes the covenant ideals of the marriage; that book needs to be used more in churches.

42 In our very confused and rebellious times, it is unfortunately necessary to point out that Proverbs clearly holds to two biological sexes. Also, "gender" matches biological sex. And right-wise desires are heterosexual and not otherwise.

43 Maybe this doesn't need to be said, but I will. My statement about healthy marriages and good sex is not intended to deny that healthy marriages can exist where, for reasons of physical malady, sex is not possible. The point is that the biblical expectation for marriage includes marriage-bed-honoring but otherwise enthusiastic sex. Seriously, Song of Songs is something else!

Chapter 8 Notes:

44 Proverbs does not speak in modern terms of employers and employees; it uses language like servant / slave and master (17:2; 25:13; 27:18; 29:19, 21; 30:10). It would be a mistake, of course, to assume that everything that governed Ancient Near East masters and slaves applies to a present-day, free society marked by at-will employment. However, the idea of one person working for and under the direction of another in the hopes of enjoying the benefits accrued to the one directing him or her certainly does apply to the subject of employment.

45 The loss and questioning of Job and the fragility of life in Ecclesiastes also provide, to the careful discipler, a wealth of material for counseling.

46 I don't know if I need to say this, but nothing I'm saying here is intended to be construed as license—no pun intended—to the claim of professional therapist. I know that most of us are not professionally trained counselors, and neither our seminary degrees nor our reading on the subject make us such. So, counsel your church members, in the sense of being there for them and point them to God, the Gospel, and Scripture, but don't assume you are a professional.

www.ingramcontent.com/pod-product-compliance
Lightning Source LLC
Chambersburg PA
CBHW031413120626
46545CB00006B/2125